FROM SEED TO SUPPER
JACKFRUIT

From Seed To Supper Jackfruit

Mack Rafeal

Noble Publishing

Contents

INDEX	1
Chapter 1	3
Chapter 2	17
Chapter 3	33
Chapter 4	50
Chapter 5	65
Chapter 6	80
Chapter 7	95

INDEX

Chapter 1: Introduction to Jackfruit
1.1 Overview of Jackfruit: A versatile tropical fruit
1.2 Historical significance and cultural importance
1.3 Nutritional value and health benefits

Chapter 2: The Jackfruit Seed: Planting the Foundation
2.1 Understanding Jackfruit seeds: Characteristics and uses
2.2 Selecting the right seeds for cultivation
2.3 Planting and germination process
2.4 Tips for successful seedling development

Chapter 3: Cultivating Jackfruit: Nurturing Growth
3.1 Ideal climate and soil conditions for Jackfruit cultivation
3.2 Choosing the right location for planting
3.3 Pruning and care for healthy tree development
3.4 Dealing with common pests and diseases

Chapter 4: Blooms of Promise: Jackfruit Blossoms and Pollination
4.1 The flowering process of Jackfruit trees
4.2 Importance of pollination for fruit development
4.3 Natural and artificial pollination methods
4.4 Maximizing fruit yield through effective pollination

Chapter 5: Fruitful Harvest: Jackfruit Development Stages
5.1 Tracking the stages of Jackfruit development
5.2 Recognizing when the fruit is ready for harvest
5.3 Harvesting techniques and tools

5.4 Post-harvest handling and storage

Chapter 6: Jackfruit in the Kitchen: Culinary Adventures

6.1 Diverse culinary uses of Jackfruit: From savory to sweet dishes
6.2 Popular traditional and modern recipes
6.3 Nutritional aspects of Jackfruit-based meals
6.4 Exploring the global popularity of Jackfruit in various cuisines

Chapter 7: Beyond the Table: Jackfruit in Sustainable Agriculture

7.1 Jackfruit as a sustainable crop: Benefits for the environment
7.2 Potential economic impact on local communities
7.3 The role of Jackfruit in agroforestry and biodiversity
7.4 Future prospects and innovations in Jackfruit cultivation

Chapter 1

Introduction to Jackfruit

Jackfruit (Artocarpus heterophyllus) is a tropical tree natural product local to southwest India. Venerated for its huge size, unmistakable smell, and flexible culinary applications, the jackfruit has earned worldwide consideration as a wonderful and practical food source. As perhaps of the biggest organic product on the planet, a solitary jackfruit can gauge as much as 80 pounds (36 kilograms) and arrive at lengths of more than three feet (one meter). The actual tree, an evergreen that has a place with the Moraceae family, flourishes in tropical marshes and is very much adjusted to locales with high temperatures and moistness.

With a captivating history going back millennia, jackfruit has been a necessary piece of the culinary and social scene in its local districts. Its development has spread across different tropical nations, including Bangladesh, Sri Lanka, Malaysia, and the Philippines. The jackfruit tree, portrayed by enormous, reflexive leaves and a straight trunk, has turned into a fundamental part of agroforestry frameworks, giving shade and food in different environments.

The jackfruit's logical name, Artocarpus heterophyllus, mirrors its assorted foliage — each leaf on the tree can display an alternate shape, a trademark that recognizes it from different species inside the Artocarpus sort. The tree bears both male and female blossoms, with the female blossoms bringing about the notable jackfruit, while the male blossoms add to the fertilization interaction. Jackfruit trees are versatile and can flourish in a scope of soil types, adding to their flexibility and broad development.

One of the unmistakable elements of jackfruit is its flexibility as a food source. The natural product is consumed at different phases of readiness, each offering an exceptional surface and flavor profile. At the point when youthful and unripe, jackfruit has a nonpartisan taste and a substantial surface, making it a well known meat substitute in veggie lover and vegetarian dishes. As it matures, the natural product changes into a sweet and fragrant delicacy, with units that are delicious and wealthy in supplements. The seeds, which are frequently disposed of, are likewise eatable and can be cooked or bubbled, introducing an extra dietary part.

Past its culinary applications, jackfruit has earned respect for tending to food security and natural challenges potential. The tree's capacity to flourish in different agroecological conditions, combined with its high return and low support prerequisites, positions jackfruit as a reasonable yield with the ability to improve livelihoods in tropical locales. Besides, the dietary wealth of jackfruit, joined with its versatility, puts forth it an important resource in attempts to battle unhealthiness and advance food power.

The excursion of jackfruit from a local staple to a worldwide peculiarity is set apart by its incorporation into different cooking styles around the world. Lately, the natural product has acquired prevalence in Western nations as a plant-based other option, praised for its capacity to mirror the surface of pulled pork or destroyed chicken when ready as an exquisite dish. From curries and stews to burgers and tacos, jackfruit's culinary flexibility has caught the creative mind of gourmet specialists and home cooks the same.

As the interest for plant-based and manageable food choices keeps on rising, jackfruit has arisen as a convincing answer for meet these developing buyer inclinations. Its status as an environment versatile yield further highlights its capability to add to worldwide food security notwithstanding environmental change. This presentation investigates the diverse idea of jackfruit, digging into its plant attributes, verifiable importance, culinary applications, and its job in addressing contemporary difficulties connected with food creation and ecological supportability.

To see the value in the meaning of jackfruit, one should dive into its organic qualities, understanding the unpredictable subtleties that add to its uniqueness. The jackfruit tree, Artocarpus heterophyllus, is essential for the Moraceae family, which likewise incorporates figs, mulberries, and breadfruit.

Native to the rainforests of the Western Ghats in southwest India, jackfruit has adjusted to a scope of heat and humidities and is presently developed in different nations with reasonable circumstances.

The jackfruit tree is an evergreen with a thick shelter of enormous, shiny leaves. Its straight trunk offers help for the huge natural products that can weigh somewhere in the range of 10 to 80 pounds. The actual leaves are unmistakable, displaying huge heterophylly — implying that leaves on a similar tree can fluctuate in shape. This special capabilities jackfruit separated from different individuals from the Artocarpus variety.

The tree produces both male and female blossoms on isolated inflorescences. The male blossoms are little and circular, while the female blossoms are bigger and situated on short, thick stalks. The female blossoms form into the notable jackfruit, and their huge size is a demonstration of the striking potential for natural product development. Fertilization is commonly worked with by bugs, permitting the tree to duplicate and yield another age of natural products.

Jackfruit's versatility to assorted soil types and agroecological conditions adds to its inescapable development. It flourishes in tropical marshes, where high temperatures and mugginess establish an optimal climate for its development. The tree's capacity to persevere through shifting soil conditions makes it a versatile harvest, fit for flourishing in various scenes. This versatility plays had a critical impact in the dispersal of jackfruit development past its local reach.

The historical backdrop of jackfruit is profoundly interwoven with the social and culinary practices of the locales where it began. Archeological proof recommends that jackfruit development has been rehearsed in southwest India for millennia, with its utilization tracing all the way back to the Vedic time frame. Over the long haul, jackfruit spread to other tropical locales, turning into a necessary piece of the culinary scene in nations like Bangladesh, Sri Lanka, Malaysia, and the Philippines.

In its local districts, jackfruit isn't only a wellspring of food however holds social and strict importance. The organic product is frequently connected with fruitfulness and flourishing, and its presence in customs and functions represents overflow. In Hinduism, jackfruit is viewed as a promising contribution, and its consideration in bubbly festivals mirrors its hallowed status. The social significance of jackfruit is further obvious in its portrayal in craftsmanship, writing, and old stories across different networks.

As jackfruit rose above its local limits, its culinary applications developed and adjusted to the assorted preferences and inclinations of various societies. In India, youthful, unripe jackfruit is a well known fixing in veggie lover dishes, valued for its capacity to retain flavors and copy the surface of meat. It is utilized in curries, sautés, and biryanis, offering a significant and protein-rich part to vegan feasts.

In Southeast Asia, especially in Indonesia and Malaysia, jackfruit is a typical fixing in customary dishes. The ready natural product is appreciated new or utilized in treats, while the youthful, green jackfruit is frequently stewed or curried. The adaptability of jackfruit in both exquisite and sweet arrangements has added to its far and wide reception in provincial cooking styles.

The Western world has likewise embraced jackfruit as of late, especially with regards to plant-based eats less. With its sinewy surface and capacity to retain flavors, youthful jackfruit has turned into a well known meat substitute in veggie lover and vegetarian dishes. From jackfruit tacos to pulled jackfruit sandwiches, imaginative gourmet specialists and home cooks have investigated its true capacity as an exquisite fixing, acquainting it with a more extensive crowd.

Jackfruit's ascent to worldwide recognition isn't exclusively founded on its culinary allure; it is likewise attached in its capability to address contemporary difficulties connected with food security and ecological manageability. As the worldwide populace proceeds to develop, and environmental change presents dangers to conventional horticulture, the requirement for versatile and maintainable food sources turns out to be progressively dire.

Jackfruit stands apart as an environment strong yield with a few credits that make it appropriate to add to food security. Its capacity to flourish in different agroecological conditions, including minimal terrains, gives adaptability in development. The tree's insignificant water prerequisites and protection from bugs add to its low upkeep, making it an appealing choice for ranchers confronting unusual climatic circumstances.

Besides, jackfruit's high return per tree is a prominent element that improves its allure as a reasonable harvest. A solitary tree can create a critical amount of natural products, giving a significant reap to both neighborhood utilization and business purposes. This viewpoint is especially urgent in areas where limited scope ranchers look for strong yields with the potential for financial reasonability.

Jackfruit's dietary profile adds one more layer to its worth as a food source. While the organic product is low in calories, it is plentiful in dietary fiber, nutrients, and minerals. Youthful jackfruit, specifically, contains an eminent measure of protein, making it an important expansion to consumes less calories, particularly in districts where lack of protein is a worry. The seeds of the jackfruit, frequently ignored, are likewise nutritious and can add to dietary variety.

The supportability of jackfruit reaches out past its healthful and agroecological angles. As a lasting yield, the jackfruit tree has a more extended life expectancy contrasted with yearly harvests, decreasing the requirement for continuous replanting. This trademark upgrades soil wellbeing, forestalls disintegration, and adds to the general flexibility of agroecosystems.

Notwithstanding its true capacity as a staple food, jackfruit offers potential open doors for esteem expansion and pay age. The handling of jackfruit into different items, like dried bites, flour, and handled food varieties, opens roads for business venture and the advancement of limited scope endeavors. This viewpoint lines up with the more extensive objective of advancing agro-handling and setting out financial open doors in rustic networks.

While jackfruit presents a convincing case for its part in practical farming and food security, challenges exist that warrant consideration. The potential for monoculture and business abuse of jackfruit raises worries about hereditary variety and the drawn out flexibility of the yield. Endeavors to advance supportable development works on, including agroforestry and coordinated bug the executives, are fundamental to relieve these dangers.

Besides, as jackfruit acquires fame in worldwide business sectors, issues connected with fair exchange, moral obtaining, and impartial circulation of advantages need cautious thought. Guaranteeing that smallholder ranchers, frequently the foundation of jackfruit development, get fair pay for their endeavors is critical for the supportable development of the jackfruit business.

All in all, the excursion of jackfruit from a territorial staple to a worldwide peculiarity highlights its importance in tending to contemporary difficulties in the domains of food security and ecological maintainability. Its herbal qualities, well established history, culinary flexibility, and potential as an environment strong harvest all in all add to its status as a wonderful natural product.

As the world wrestles with the intricacies of taking care of a developing populace while relieving the effects of environmental change, jackfruit arises as an encouraging sign — an image of strength and flexibility notwithstanding challenges. Its mix into different cooking styles and its allure as a plant-based elective mirror a more extensive change in shopper inclinations toward reasonable and nutritious food choices.

As we proceed to investigate and tackle the capability of jackfruit, it is basic to move toward its development and usage with a comprehensive point of view, considering natural, social, and financial aspects. Thusly, we can completely open the advantages of this exceptional organic product, adding to a more supportable and evenhanded future for worldwide food frameworks. Jackfruit, with its gigantic presence and heap prospects, welcomes us to reconsider our relationship with food and develop a more amicable concurrence with the normal world.

1.1 Overview of Jackfruit: A versatile tropical fruit

Jackfruit (Artocarpus heterophyllus) remains as a demonstration of the uncommon variety and lavishness tracked down in tropical organic products. Starting from the rainforests of southwest India, this goliath natural product has accumulated consideration worldwide for its noteworthy size, unmistakable fragrance, and multi-layered culinary applications. As an individual from the Moraceae family, the jackfruit tree, logically known as Artocarpus heterophyllus, has a place with similar family as figs, mulberries, and breadfruit.

Its flexibility to different heat and humidities, combined with its flexibility in both exquisite and sweet dishes, has raised jackfruit to an unmistakable situation in the domain of worldwide cooking.

Naturally, the jackfruit tree is an evergreen with a striking appearance. Its huge, lustrous leaves show critical heterophylly, a component that separates it inside the Artocarpus family. This trademark implies that leaves on a similar tree can differ in shape, adding to the visual interest of the tree. The storage compartment is straight and solid, offering help for the enormous organic products that can arrive at shocking loads of as much as 80 pounds (36 kilograms). The tree produces both male and female blossoms on discrete inflorescences, with the female blossoms leading to the famous jackfruit.

By and large, jackfruit has been a staple in the eating routine of networks in southwest India for millennia. Archeological proof focuses to its development during the Vedic time frame, and its importance rises above simple food — it is woven into the social and strict texture of the district. With relationship to richness and thriving, jackfruit has turned into a vital piece of customs and functions, representing overflow and favorability.

As jackfruit navigated geographic limits, its culinary applications advanced to suit the inclinations of different societies. In India, youthful, unripe jackfruit is a leaned toward fixing in vegan dishes, eminent for its capacity to retain enhances and give a substantial surface. In Southeast Asia, both ready and unripe jackfruit track down their direction into conventional recipes, offering a range of flavors from sweet to exquisite. All the more as of late, jackfruit has acquired prevalence in the West as a plant-based meat substitute, praised for its sinewy surface and flexibility in flavorful arrangements.

The worldwide hug of jackfruit reaches out past its culinary appeal. With the rising accentuation on feasible and plant-based counts calories, jackfruit has arisen as a convincing answer for address contemporary difficulties connected with food security and ecological supportability. Its strength in different agroecological conditions, high return per tree, and healthful lavishness add to its true capacity as a reasonable yield with the ability to upgrade vocations and advance food power.

From a natural stance, jackfruit trees show surprising flexibility to different heat and humidities. Flourishing in districts portrayed by high temperatures and stickiness, the tree's capacity to persevere through various soil conditions adds to its strength. Its flexibility has worked with its spread to nations like Bangladesh, Sri Lanka, Malaysia, and the Philippines, making it a huge part of agroforestry frameworks in different biological systems.

The flexibility of jackfruit as a food source is a characterizing highlight that separates it from numerous different natural products. The natural product can be consumed at different phases of readiness, each stage offering a particular culinary encounter. In its young and unripe state, jackfruit has an unbiased taste and a substantial surface, making it an optimal element for exquisite dishes. As it ages, the natural product changes, turning out to be sweet and fragrant, with delicious units that are appreciated new or integrated into treats.

The seeds of the jackfruit, frequently ignored, are additionally consumable and nutritious. Cooked or heated up, these seeds add a healthy component to the jackfruit's culinary collection. The seeds, alongside the organic product's tissue, add to the by and large nourishing profile of jackfruit, making it a significant option to eats less carbs in locales where lack of protein is a worry.

Jackfruit's excursion from a territorial staple to a worldwide sensation is set apart by its joining into different cooking styles around the world. Its reception in Western nations, specifically, grandstands its versatility and appeal to different palates. From jackfruit burgers to tacos and curries, gourmet experts and home cooks the same have embraced its culinary potential, situating it as a flexible and maintainable fixing.

The worldwide shift toward plant-based consumes less calories and feasible food decisions has additionally impelled jackfruit into the spotlight. As a meat substitute, especially in veggie lover and vegetarian dishes, jackfruit offers a surface suggestive of pulled pork or destroyed chicken. This trademark has prompted its fuse into a large number of flavorful recipes, growing its span and ubiquity among those looking for plant-based other options.

Be that as it may, jackfruit's importance stretches out past its culinary applications. Despite environmental change and the requirement for strong and maintainable food sources, jackfruit stands apart as an environment tough yield. Its flexibility to differing agroecological conditions, negligible water necessities, and protection from bothers add to its low upkeep and appropriateness for development in assorted scenes.

The high return per jackfruit tree is an eminent element that upgrades its allure as a supportable yield. A solitary tree can deliver a significant amount of organic products, giving a huge reap to both neighborhood utilization and business purposes. This perspective is especially vital in areas where limited scope ranchers look for strong harvests with the potential for monetary practicality.

The wholesome lavishness of jackfruit adds one more layer to its allure as a reasonable food source. While the organic product is low in calories, it is plentiful in dietary fiber, nutrients, and minerals.

Youthful jackfruit, specifically, contains a remarkable measure of protein, making it an important expansion to consumes less calories, particularly in locales where lack of protein is a worry. The seeds of the jackfruit, frequently disposed of, are likewise nutritious and can add to dietary variety.

The supportability of jackfruit development goes past its wholesome and agroecological perspectives. As a lasting yield, the jackfruit tree has a more extended life expectancy contrasted with yearly harvests, lessening the requirement for continuous replanting. This trademark improves soil wellbeing, forestalls disintegration, and adds to the general versatility of agroecosystems.

Notwithstanding its true capacity as a staple food, jackfruit offers potential open doors for esteem expansion and pay age. Handling jackfruit into different items, like dried bites, flour, and handled food varieties, opens roads for business and the improvement of limited scope undertakings. This lines up with more extensive objectives of advancing agro-handling and setting out financial open doors in country networks.

In any case, as the ubiquity of jackfruit develops, challenges arise that require cautious thought. The potential for monoculture and business double-dealing of jackfruit raises worries about hereditary variety and the drawn out strength of the yield. Endeavors to advance maintainable development works on, including agroforestry and incorporated bother the executives, are fundamental to relieve these dangers and guarantee the life span of jackfruit as a supportable harvest.

Also, issues connected with fair exchange, moral obtaining, and impartial appropriation of advantages come to the front as jackfruit enters worldwide business sectors. Guaranteeing that smallholder ranchers, frequently the foundation of jackfruit development, get fair pay for their endeavors is critical for the practical development of the jackfruit business. Offsetting commercialization with moral contemplations becomes basic in encouraging an industry that isn't just monetarily feasible yet additionally socially and ecologically capable.

All in all, the outline of jackfruit uncovers a product of enormous potential and importance with regards to worldwide food frameworks. Its organic qualities, verifiable roots, culinary flexibility, and job in tending to contemporary difficulties by and large position jackfruit as an exceptional and diverse tropical natural product.

As the world wrestles with the intricacies of taking care of a developing populace while moderating the effects of environmental change, jackfruit arises as an image of strength and flexibility. Its reconciliation into different cooking styles and its allure as a plant-based elective mirror a more extensive change in buyer inclinations toward feasible and nutritious food choices.

The excursion of jackfruit from a provincial staple to a worldwide peculiarity welcomes us to reevaluate our relationship with food and the regular world. As we investigate and tackle the capability of jackfruit, it becomes clear that this flexible tropical organic product has the ability to contribute fundamentally to an additional supportable and evenhanded future. Jackfruit, with its goliath presence and horde prospects, urges us to embrace development, equilibrium, and amicability in our way to deal with food creation and utilization.

1.2 Historical significance and cultural importance

The verifiable importance and social significance of jackfruit length centuries, winding around a rich embroidery that mirrors the profound associations among individuals and this tropical organic product. Starting in the rainforests of southwest India, jackfruit's development goes back millennia, making a permanent imprint on the culinary and social customs of the locales where it flourished.

Archeological proof focuses to the Vedic time frame as the beginning stage of jackfruit development in southwest India. Its presence in antiquated texts and sacred writings validates its well established relationship with the social texture of the district. As people group participated in farming practices, the jackfruit tree turned into an essential part of their environments, giving food, conceal, and adding to the horticultural biodiversity of the scene.

Past its job as a staple food, jackfruit obtained social and strict importance in the customs of its local districts. The organic product's relationship with richness and thriving raised it to an image of overflow and promise. In Hinduism, jackfruit tracked down a spot in customs and services, where its presence connoted favors and favorable luck. The social significance of jackfruit showed in strict practices as well as in workmanship, writing, and legends, where it turned into a theme addressing life, development, and imperativeness.

Jackfruit's process past its local areas unfurled as shipping lanes extended, working with the trading of merchandise and social practices. First experience with various tropical nations, including Bangladesh, Sri Lanka, Malaysia, and the Philippines, saw the organic product absorb into different culinary practices, every area imbuing its novel flavors and methods into the arrangement of jackfruit-based dishes.

In India, where jackfruit has a well established history, it turned into a necessary piece of veggie lover cooking. The youthful, unripe jackfruit, with its unbiased taste and substantial surface, arose as a leaned toward fixing in flavorful dishes. From curries and pan-sears to biryanis and bites, jackfruit displayed its culinary flexibility, adjusting to the different palates and inclinations of the Indian subcontinent.

Southeast Asia embraced jackfruit with equivalent excitement, coordinating it into customary recipes. The ready organic product tracked down its direction into treats, while the youthful, green jackfruit turned into a critical part in flavorful stews and curries. The versatility of jackfruit to different culinary styles and arrangements added to its broad acknowledgment, and it turned into a culinary symbol in the locale.

As jackfruit rose above geological limits, its culinary applications kept on developing. Lately, especially in Western nations, jackfruit has acquired prominence as a plant-based meat substitute. The stringy surface of youthful jackfruit, joined with its capacity to retain flavors, made it a sought-after fixing in veggie lover and vegetarian dishes. From pulled jackfruit sandwiches to tacos and burgers, jackfruit's flexibility tracked down another crowd anxious to investigate manageable and plant-based other options.

The social significance of jackfruit reaches out past its culinary applications. In India, the wood of the jackfruit tree has been generally utilized for development and carpentry. The lumber's sturdiness and protection from termites make it an important asset, adding to the supportable utilization of the whole jackfruit tree. This double reason usage further features the fundamental job of jackfruit in the day to day routines and practices of networks.

In the Philippines, jackfruit holds social importance during the festival of the Moriones Celebration. The organic product is utilized as a prop and represents overflow during the celebration, adding a merry and shared aspect to the social practices related with jackfruit.

Jackfruit's imagery in social and strict settings is likewise reflected in the craftsmanship and writing of different networks. In compositions, models, and writing, jackfruit is much of the time portrayed as an image of life, development, and success. The organic product's relationship with overflow and promise is repetitive in creative articulations, underlining its persevering through influence on the aggregate creative mind of social orders.

The verifiable excursion of jackfruit interweaves with human movement, exchange, and social trade. As the organic product spread to various regions of the planet, it turned into an extension interfacing different networks through a common appreciation for its flavors and social importance. In this globalized setting, jackfruit fills in as a sign of the interconnectedness of societies and the capacity of food to rise above limits.

As jackfruit acquires unmistakable quality in contemporary culinary scenes, endeavors to safeguard and advance its social legacy become pivotal. In its local areas, drives to archive conventional recipes, culinary strategies, and social practices connected with jackfruit add to the protection of its social legacy. Moreover, the trading of culinary information and encounters on a worldwide scale cultivates an appreciation for the social variety implanted in jackfruit's culinary excursion.

While jackfruit's prevalence in worldwide business sectors develops, moving toward its development and utilization with aversion to social nuances is fundamental. Fair exchange rehearses, moral obtaining, and regard for conventional information are necessary to guaranteeing that the advantages of jackfruit's worldwide allure are shared impartially with the networks that have developed and esteemed it for a really long time.

All in all, the verifiable importance and social significance of jackfruit are well established in the scenes, customs, and minds of the networks that have developed and celebrated it for centuries. From its beginnings in the rainforests of southwest India to its joining into different worldwide cooking styles, jackfruit has turned into an image of overflow, flexibility, and interconnectedness. As we relish its flavors and investigate its culinary potential, it is basic to perceive and respect the social legacy that goes with this adaptable tropical natural product. Jackfruit welcomes us to see the value in not exclusively its taste and surface yet additionally the rich woven artwork of stories, ceremonies, and customs that have made it a persevering through symbol in the worldwide culinary scene.

1.3 Nutritional value and health benefits

The healthy benefit and medical advantages of jackfruit add to its standing as a tasty natural product as well as an important part of a sound and adjusted diet. Loaded with fundamental supplements and offering a scope of wellbeing advancing properties, jackfruit has procured its status as a nutritious force to be reckoned with the possibility to address different dietary requirements and wellbeing concerns.

One of the key credits that make jackfruit healthfully critical is its rich arrangement of nutrients and minerals. Jackfruit is a decent wellspring of L-ascorbic acid, a strong cell reinforcement known for its job in helping the resistant framework, advancing skin wellbeing, and supporting the body's capacity to retain iron. The presence of different nutrients, including vitamin A, vitamin B6, and folate, further upgrades the nourishing profile of jackfruit, adding to generally speaking prosperity.

Notwithstanding its nutrient substance, jackfruit is a mineral-rich natural product. It contains fundamental minerals like potassium, magnesium, and manganese. Potassium assumes a vital part in keeping up with legitimate heart capability, controlling pulse, and supporting muscle and nerve capability. Magnesium is engaged with bone wellbeing, energy digestion, and muscle constrictions, while manganese adds to cell reinforcement protection and bone development.

Dietary fiber is another champion element of jackfruit's nourishing creation. Fiber is fundamental for stomach related wellbeing, advancing customary defecations and forestalling blockage. The fiber content in jackfruit adds to a sensation of completion, which might help with weight the board by decreasing by and large calorie consumption.

Besides, an eating routine wealthy in fiber is related with a lower hazard of creating conditions like coronary illness and type 2 diabetes.

A fascinating part of jackfruit's dietary profile is its protein content. While organic products are not normally high in protein, jackfruit stands apart for its generally higher protein content contrasted with different organic products. This makes it an important expansion to veggie lover and vegetarian eats less carbs, giving a plant-based wellspring of protein. The protein in jackfruit contains different amino acids, adding to the body's protein needs.

Aside from the healthful parts found in the tissue of the natural product, jackfruit seeds are likewise a wellspring of supplements. These seeds are wealthy in protein, solid fats, and dietary fiber. Broiling or bubbling jackfruit seeds makes them a nutritious and delectable tidbit. Counting jackfruit seeds in the eating routine adds an additional aspect to the wholesome advantages got from this flexible tropical natural product.

The dietary wealth of jackfruit lines up with its capability to address explicit wellbeing concerns. As a low-calorie and supplement thick food, jackfruit can be an important expansion to weight the board techniques. The fiber content adds to satiety, helping people feel full and happy with more modest parts, which can be valuable for those intending to accomplish or keep a solid weight.

The potassium content in jackfruit is important for its part in supporting cardiovascular wellbeing. Potassium manages circulatory strain by balancing the impacts of sodium and advancing vasodilation, which can add to a lower chance of hypertension and related cardiovascular issues. Counting potassium-rich food sources like jackfruit in the eating routine backings in general heart wellbeing.

The presence of cancer prevention agents in jackfruit further upgrades its potential medical advantages. Cell reinforcements assume a pivotal part in killing free revolutionaries in the body, which can add to oxidative pressure and irritation. Persistent irritation is related with different ailments, including coronary illness, diabetes, and certain tumors. The cell reinforcement properties of jackfruit add to decreasing oxidative pressure and aggravation, advancing generally wellbeing and prosperity.

Jackfruit's effect on glucose levels is one more area of interest for those with diabetes or in danger of fostering the condition. The fiber content in jackfruit, joined with its moderately low glycemic record, can add to more readily glucose control. The steady arrival of glucose into the circulatory system forestalls sharp spikes and crashes in glucose levels, making jackfruit an ideal choice for people overseeing diabetes or insulin obstruction.

Additionally, the dietary fiber in jackfruit adds to stomach related wellbeing. An eating routine high in fiber upholds standard defecations, forestalls clogging, and advances a solid stomach microbiota. The prebiotic properties of fiber in jackfruit give fuel to helpful stomach microscopic organisms, adding to a reasonable and flourishing stomach environment. A sound stomach microbiota is related with further developed processing, supplement ingestion, and generally speaking safe capability.

Jackfruit's healthful profile likewise pursues it a reasonable decision for people following veggie lover or vegetarian eats less. Its protein content, joined with fundamental nutrients and minerals, offers a plant-based wellspring of supplements that can assist with meeting the wholesome prerequisites of those swearing off creature items. The flexibility of jackfruit in flavorful dishes further positions it as a significant meat substitute in plant-based eats less.

While the healthy benefit and medical advantages of jackfruit are significant, it means a lot to take note of that singular dietary necessities and wellbeing contemplations fluctuate. Likewise with any food, control and equilibrium are critical. Counting different supplement rich food sources as a feature of a balanced eating regimen is fundamental for in general wellbeing.

All in all, the healthy benefit and medical advantages of jackfruit make it a champion organic product in the domain of worldwide cooking. From its rich substance of nutrients and minerals to its fiber and protein commitments, jackfruit offers a range of supplements that line up with different dietary requirements. Whether as a tasty expansion to flavorful dishes or a sweet and delicious natural product delighted in new, jackfruit's flexibility reaches out past the culinary domain to add to in general prosperity. As dietary inclinations shift toward plant-put together choices and a concentration with respect to wellbeing cognizant decisions, jackfruit arises as a convincing and nutritious decision, welcoming people to enjoy not exclusively its taste yet in addition the horde medical advantages it offers that would be useful.

Jackfruit, the tropical goliath with its great size and particular flavor, entices the taste buds as well as offers a scope of medical advantages that make it a wholesome force to be reckoned with. From its rich cluster of nutrients and minerals to its vital commitments to stomach related wellbeing, heart wellbeing, and diabetes the executives, jackfruit stands apart as something other than a delightful expansion to dinners — a flexible organic product upholds generally prosperity.

1. **Supplement Rich Creation:**
   Jackfruit flaunts an amazing wholesome profile, highlighting fundamental nutrients and minerals that add to generally wellbeing. It is a rich wellspring of L-ascorbic acid, a cell reinforcement known for its invulnerable helping properties and backing for skin wellbeing. Furthermore, jackfruit gives a range of B nutrients, including vitamin B6 and folate, fundamental for

different physical processes, including digestion and the development of red platelets.

2. **Dietary Fiber for Stomach related Wellbeing:**
   One of the champion elements of jackfruit is its high fiber content. Dietary fiber is essential for stomach related wellbeing, advancing normal defecations and forestalling clogging. The fiber in jackfruit adds mass to the stool, helping with smooth processing and supporting a solid gastrointestinal framework. Integrating fiber-rich food sources like jackfruit into the eating routine adds to ideal stomach related capability.

3. **Weight The board Backing:**
   Jackfruit's fiber content assumes a part in weight the executives by advancing a sensation of totality and diminishing generally speaking calorie consumption. As a low-calorie, supplement thick food, jackfruit can be an important expansion to techniques pointed toward accomplishing or keeping a solid weight. The fiber content adds to satiety, assisting people with controling gorging and pursue careful food decisions.

4. **Heart Medical advantages:**
   Potassium, a critical mineral tracked down in jackfruit, is fundamental to heart wellbeing. Potassium controls pulse by balancing the impacts of sodium and advancing vasodilation. Keeping up with ideal pulse levels is fundamental for cardiovascular wellbeing, and including potassium-rich food varieties like jackfruit in the eating regimen upholds this critical part of heart capability. The heart-solid properties of jackfruit add to generally cardiovascular prosperity.

5. **Cell reinforcement Properties:**
   Jackfruit is wealthy in cell reinforcements, which assume a fundamental part in killing free extremists in the body. Free extremists add to oxidative pressure, which, whenever left uncontrolled, can prompt irritation and different ongoing circumstances. The cancer prevention agents in jackfruit assist with alleviating oxidative pressure, offering security against cell harm and supporting by and large wellbeing.

6. **Glucose Guideline:**
   For people overseeing diabetes or those in danger of fostering the condition, jackfruit's effect on glucose levels is quite compelling. The fiber content, joined with its somewhat low glycemic record, adds to more readily glucose control. The steady arrival of glucose into the circulation system forestalls sharp spikes and crashes in glucose levels, making jackfruit a great choice for those expecting to oversee diabetes or insulin opposition.

7. **Protein Content for Veggie lover and Vegetarian Diets:**
   While natural products are not commonly high in protein, jackfruit stands apart for its somewhat higher protein content contrasted with different

organic products. This makes it a significant expansion to veggie lover and vegetarian eats less carbs, giving a plant-based wellspring of protein.

The amino acids present in jackfruit add to the body's protein needs, supporting muscle capability and generally speaking protein necessities for those keeping away from creature items.

8. **Stomach Wellbeing and Microbiota Backing:**

    The dietary fiber in jackfruit adds to stomach related wellbeing by supporting a flourishing stomach microbiota. The prebiotic properties of fiber give fuel to valuable stomach microscopic organisms, advancing a reasonable and various stomach environment. A solid stomach microbiota is related with further developed processing, supplement ingestion, and generally speaking invulnerable capability. Remembering jackfruit for the eating routine adds a positive aspect to destroy wellbeing.

9. **Supplement Thick Nibbling with Jackfruit Seeds:**

    Jackfruit seeds, frequently disposed of, are a healthful force to be reckoned with. These seeds are wealthy in protein, sound fats, and dietary fiber. Cooking or bubbling jackfruit seeds transforms them into a nutritious and scrumptious tidbit. Counting jackfruit seeds in the eating routine adds an additional layer of dietary advantages, offering a helpful and supplement thick choice for those hoping to expand the medical advantages of the whole natural product.

10. **Adaptable Culinary Applications for Smart dieting:**

The adaptability of jackfruit in the kitchen adds to its potential medical advantages. From exquisite dishes like curries and pan-sears to sweet treats and bites, jackfruit's flexibility permits it to be integrated into different recipes. This flexibility urges people to investigate innovative and nutritious culinary choices, making it simpler to incorporate jackfruit into a balanced and wellbeing cognizant eating routine.

Taking everything into account, the medical advantages of jackfruit reach out a long ways past its delicious taste. From its supplement rich organization to its help for stomach related wellbeing, heart wellbeing, and diabetes the executives, jackfruit arises as a natural product that fulfills culinary desires as well as adds to in general prosperity. Whether delighted in new, as a meat substitute in exquisite dishes, or as a nutritious nibble with cooked seeds, jackfruit welcomes people to relish its flavors while procuring the various wellbeing benefits it offers that would be useful. As dietary inclinations keep on developing towards cognizant and plant-based decisions, jackfruit remains as a healthy choice that lines up with the more extensive objective of encouraging a solid and adjusted way of life.

Chapter 2

The Jackfruit Seed: Planting the Foundation

Quite a long time ago, in a curious town settled between moving slopes and lavish plant life, there existed a practice well established in the core of the local area. This custom was based on the modest jackfruit seed, an apparently immaterial component of the town's normal abundance. Little did the residents had at least some idea that these seeds held the way in to a feasible future and would assume a urgent part in forming the fate of their local area.

The town, known for its affectionate local area and maintainable practices, had for some time been reliant upon agribusiness for its occupation. Ages had developed the land, passing down their insight and customs to guarantee the success of the town. Notwithstanding, as time walked forward, the town confronted difficulties that tried the versatility of its farming practices.

The changing environment brought eccentric weather conditions, testing the conventional harvests that had been the backbone of the local area for quite a long time. The seniors of the town, shrewd and experienced, perceived the requirement for transformation. It was during one such assembling of the town chamber that an old rancher named Keshav talked enthusiastically about the jackfruit seeds - a fortune inconspicuous.

Keshav, endured by long stretches of work in the fields, remained before the board with a flicker of assurance in his eyes. He discussed the jackfruit tree, a durable monster that graced the scene with its wide leaves and forcing presence. The jackfruit, an enormous and flexible natural product, was notable in the locale for its dietary benefit and culinary purposes. Notwithstanding, it was the unassuming seed that Keshav trusted held the possibility to change the town's fortunes.

"These seeds," Keshav shouted, holding a modest bunch of them in his twisted hands, "are something beyond the leftovers of a scrumptious natural product. They are the groundwork of flexibility, the way in to our horticultural future. We should establish them, support them, and watch as they develop into trees that won't just support us yet in addition shield our property from the difficulties that lie ahead."

The chamber listened eagerly, their countenances mirroring a combination of incredulity and interest. Keshav's vision, be that as it may, reverberated with a portion of the more moderate personalities among them. They saw a chance to enhance the town's harvests, to embrace a plant that could endure the vulnerabilities of an evolving environment.

Thus, the excursion of the jackfruit seed started. Keshav, filled by an enthusiasm to get the eventual fate of his local area, mobilized a gathering of youthful ranchers to go along with him in this undertaking. They set off to accumulate jackfruit seeds from the trees dissipated across the town, leaving on a mission that wouldn't just change the scene yet in addition the existences of the people who hoped against hope.

The method involved with establishing the jackfruit seeds required persistence and devotion. The youthful ranchers, directed by Keshav's insight, arranged the dirt with care, guaranteeing it was ripe and appropriate for the seeds to flourish. As they sowed each seed, they imagined a future where the jackfruit trees would stand tall, giving shade and food to ages yet unborn.

Seasons passed, and the jackfruit seeds grew into saplings, their delicate shoots aiming high. The town, once doubtful, started to observe the change occurring. The jackfruit trees, with their strong trunks and wide overhangs, flourished in the town's dirt. They endured storms and endured dry seasons, ending up the versatile power that Keshav had imagined.

As the trees developed, so did the advantages they brought to the local area. The jackfruit, with its wealth of nutritious tissue, turned into a staple in the locals' weight control plans. It gave food during seasons of shortage and turned into an image of strength notwithstanding misfortune. The once-suspicious residents currently viewed the jackfruit trees with appreciation, remembering them as watchmen of their prosperity.

Yet, the effect of the jackfruit trees stretched out past simple food. Keshav, consistent with his vision, had anticipated the ecological advantages they could offer. The broad root foundations of the trees forestalled soil disintegration, mooring the rich dirt and shielding the land from debasement. The leaves gave a characteristic mulch, improving the dirt and advancing biodiversity.

Expression of the town's prosperity with jackfruit development spread, catching the consideration of adjoining networks confronting comparative difficulties. Before long, delegates from neighboring towns visited, anxious to gain from the insight of Keshav and his kindred ranchers. The town, once segregated, turned into a center point of information and development, with the jackfruit trees at the focal point of this rural insurgency.

As the development picked up speed, specialists and researchers paid heed. They concentrated on the jackfruit trees, dissecting their hereditary cosmetics and figuring out the components that made them tough notwithstanding natural pressure. The unassuming jackfruit seed, once neglected, turned into the subject of logical request, opening additional opportunities for economical farming in districts wrestling with environmental change.

The outcome of the jackfruit project likewise had social and financial ramifications for the town. The ranchers who had embraced this drive wound up at the front of a thriving green economy. The offer of jackfruit and its results turned into a type of revenue, engaging the local area to put resources into schooling, medical services, and framework. The once-battling town presently remained as a demonstration of the groundbreaking force of economical farming.

The account of the jackfruit seed spread all over, catching the creative mind of individuals all over the planet. It turned into an image of trust, an update that even notwithstanding difficulty, nature gave arrangements whenever moved toward regard and understanding. The town, once known for its separation, presently invited guests from far off lands, all anxious to observe the wonder of the jackfruit trees and gain from the insight of the people who had sowed the seeds of progress.

Amidst this freshly discovered thriving, Keshav, the old rancher whose vision had started the change, remained under the shade of a transcending jackfruit tree. He wondered about the organic products swinging from its branches, pondering the excursion that had carried the town to this point. His eyes, loaded up with a feeling of satisfaction, met those of the kids playing underneath the tree - an age that would acquire the tradition of flexibility and supportability.

The outcome of the jackfruit project, nonetheless, was not without its difficulties. As the town stood out and honors, there arose a sensitive harmony between protecting the embodiment of the local area and embracing the open doors that accompanied acknowledgment. The elderly folks, including Keshav, wrested with the obligation of defending their customs while exploring the requests of an impacting world.

One of the key difficulties was keeping up with the trustworthiness of the jackfruit development despite business interests. The interest for jackfruit and its items had flooded, drawing in organizations anxious to profit by the progress of the town. The older folks, directed by a feeling of watchfulness, pondered on the most proficient method to figure out some kind of harmony between monetary development and the protection of their social legacy.

Because of these difficulties, the town chamber executed a bunch of rules to guarantee maintainable practices in jackfruit development. They energized dependable reaping, underscoring the significance of keeping up with the environmental equilibrium that had made the venture a triumph. The seniors, drawing on the insight of their predecessors, tried to make a model of manageable improvement that could be reproduced without compromising the respectability of the land.

As the town explored the intricacies of adjusting custom and progress, the jackfruit trees kept on remaining as quiet observers to the developing scene. Their branches, weighed down with organic products, influenced in the breeze, a demonstration of the agreeable conjunction of nature and human undertaking. The progress of the undertaking, established in the unassuming jackfruit seed, turned into a reference point of motivation for networks confronting comparative difficulties around the world.

The groundbreaking excursion of the jackfruit seed didn't be ignored by policymakers and preservationists. The town turned into a contextual investigation, refered to in conversations on practical horticulture and environment strength. Legislatures and non-benefit associations contacted gain from the encounters of the local area, trying to recreate the model in districts where the effect of environmental change undermined food security and vocations.

The progress of the jackfruit project likewise ignited discussions about the significance of customary information in tending to contemporary difficulties. The seniors, who had protected the insight gone down through ages, wound up at the very front of a development to perceive and regard native practices. Their accounts turned into an energizing sob for the safeguarding of social variety and the job of neighborhood networks in molding a supportable future.

As the town turned into a worldwide image of versatility, the difficulties it confronted took on another aspect. The deluge of guests, while bringing monetary open doors, likewise represented the gamble of social weakening. The older folks, insightful and knowing, wrestled with the need to impart their insight to the world while defending the sacredness of their customs.

Because of these worries, the town laid out a social trade program, welcoming people and gatherings from various regions of the planet to encounter the rich embroidery of their legacy.

The program stressed common picking up, empowering guests to share their own practices while regarding the interesting character of the town. This approach encouraged understanding as well as reinforced the connections between the town and the worldwide local area.

The jackfruit project, when a neighborhood drive brought about for a specific need, had turned into a worldwide development. The seeds planted by Keshav and his kindred ranchers had borne organic product as well as dispersed new seeds of motivation across borders. The world focused on the town for farming arrangements as well as a wellspring of trust and an update that feasible practices could be both old and imaginative.

As the years passed, the youngsters who had played underneath the jackfruit trees developed into the stewards of the land. They conveyed forward the tradition of their predecessors, sustaining the trees with the very love and care that had been imparted in them. The town, while embracing progress, remained profoundly associated with its foundations, tracking down strength in the getting through connection among nature and humankind.

The tale of the jackfruit seed, once restricted to the limits of a little town, reverberated across the pages of history. It discussed versatility, development, and the significant effect that a solitary thought could have on the direction of a local area and, likewise, the world. The jackfruit trees, standing tall and glad, demonstrated the veracity of the steadily evolving scene, a demonstration of the persevering through force of nature and the human soul.

2.1 Understanding Jackfruit seeds: Characteristics and uses

Jackfruit, the goliath tropical organic product with a particular spiky outside, has acquired prominence for its sweet and tasty tissue as well as for its flexible seeds. Frequently ignored and disposed of, jackfruit seeds are an unlikely treasure loaded with supplements and potential. Understanding the qualities and utilizations of jackfruit seeds uncovers an abundance of opportunities for culinary, dietary, and, surprisingly, monetary applications.

From the get go, jackfruit seeds could seem genuine, with a smooth, light earthy colored outside. These seeds are regularly oval or circular in shape, and their size changes relying upon the size of the jackfruit. Separating the seeds from the organic product can be a piece work serious, as they are settled inside the stringy tissue of the jackfruit. When isolated, the seeds can be bubbled or simmered to make them more attractive and simpler to strip.

The healthful profile of jackfruit seeds is noteworthy, making them an important expansion to counts calories all over the planet. Wealthy in protein, sound fats, and dietary fiber, these seeds add to a balanced and nutritious feast. They are especially eminent for their protein content, offering a plant-based protein source that can be gainful for veggie lovers and vegetarians.

Past their macronutrient piece, jackfruit seeds are a decent wellspring of micronutrients. They contain fundamental minerals like potassium, magnesium, and phosphorus, adding to in general wellbeing and prosperity. Moreover, jackfruit seeds brag cell reinforcements, which assume a urgent part in killing unsafe free revolutionaries in the body and advancing cell wellbeing.

One of the main traits of jackfruit seeds is their bland surface when cooked. This quality makes them flexible in different culinary applications. Bubbled jackfruit seeds, when cooked to a delicate consistency, can be delighted in all alone or integrated into exquisite dishes. Cooking the seeds adds a nutty flavor and crunchy surface, making them a great tidbit.

In many societies, particularly in pieces of Asia and Africa where jackfruit is bountiful, these seeds are utilized in conventional recipes. In India, for instance, jackfruit seed curry is a famous dish. The seeds are cooked with flavors, coconut, and different fixings to make a delightful and good curry that matches well with rice or bread. In Brazil, jackfruit seeds are much of the time utilized in a dish called "farofa," a delightful combination of simmered seeds, cassava flour, and flavors.

The culinary utilizations of jackfruit seeds stretch out past exquisite dishes. At the point when ground into a flour-like consistency, jackfruit seeds can be utilized as a sans gluten elective in baking. This jackfruit seed flour can be integrated into recipes for bread, flapjacks, or other heated products, giving a nutritious turn to customary flour-based things.

Jackfruit seeds additionally can possibly be handled into different items, opening additional opportunities for the food business. The extraction of jackfruit seed oil, for example, yields an oil with possible applications in cooking and as a restorative fixing. The oil contains unsaturated fats that add to its healthy benefit and may have medical advantages when consumed with some restraint.

As the culinary world finds the capability of jackfruit seeds, gourmet experts and home cooks the same are exploring different avenues regarding creative ways of integrating them into many dishes. From soups and stews to tidbits and pastries, jackfruit seeds are arising as a flexible and nutritious fixing that adds a one of a kind contort to conventional recipes.

Past their culinary purposes, jackfruit seeds stand out for their potential medical advantages. Research proposes that the bioactive mixtures present in jackfruit seeds might have cell reinforcement, mitigating, and against malignant growth properties. While additional examinations are expected to completely comprehend the degree of these advantages, the underlying discoveries feature the likely job of jackfruit seeds in advancing wellbeing and forestalling specific sicknesses.

The fiber content in jackfruit seeds adds to stomach related wellbeing by advancing standard defecations and forestalling obstruction. Also, the seeds' cancer prevention agent properties might assist with safeguarding cells from harm, supporting by and large cell wellbeing. As established researchers dives further into the nourishing and wellbeing related parts of jackfruit seeds, the seeds' status is moving from disregarded result to a significant part of a reasonable and sound eating routine.

Jackfruit seeds are not restricted to the domain of sustenance and culinary expressions; they likewise have useful applications in farming. The seeds can be utilized to proliferate jackfruit trees, adding to the supportability and development of this tropical natural product. Ranchers who perceive the capability of jackfruit seeds as an asset for both food and horticulture are doing whatever it takes to bridle their advantages for a bigger scope.

Spread of jackfruit trees from seeds includes choosing mature seeds from a solid natural product, getting them improve germination, and establishing them in reasonable circumstances. As the seeds sprout and develop into saplings, they can be relocated to their last areas, adding to the extension of jackfruit plantations. This reasonable practice guarantees the coherence of jackfruit development and permits ranchers to bridle the monetary capability of the whole jackfruit tree.

The monetary effect of jackfruit seeds reaches out past customary cultivating rehearses. Business visionaries and trailblazers are investigating ways of commercializing jackfruit seeds and their side-effects. From the development of jackfruit seed flour to the extraction of oil for corrective and culinary purposes, organizations are perceiving the undiscovered capacity of this frequently disregarded asset.

Notwithstanding its financial advantages, the development and usage of jackfruit seeds line up with feasible agribusiness rehearses. The trees flourish in different agroecological settings, giving a type of revenue to ranchers while adding to natural protection. The strength of jackfruit trees in unfriendly circumstances, for example, dry spell or unfortunate soil quality, further positions them as a significant resource for networks confronting horticultural difficulties.

The excursion of understanding jackfruit seeds rises above their nearby applications. It includes an all encompassing way to deal with feasible living, consolidating healthful, farming, and monetary aspects. The seeds, when thought about simple leftovers of a tropical organic product, have arisen as impetuses for positive change, typifying the potential for amicable concurrence among people and the regular world.

As the worldwide local area wrestles with difficulties connected with food security, ecological supportability, and wellbeing, the account of jackfruit seeds offers important experiences. It supports a change in context, encouraging people, networks, and ventures to reconsider the

likely inside apparently customary components of nature. The excursion of understanding jackfruit seeds is an update that answers for complex issues frequently lie in the many-sided connections among people and the climate.

2.2 Selecting the right seeds for cultivation

Choosing the right seeds for development is a principal and essential move toward the excursion of any rancher or nursery worker. The selection of seeds sets the establishment for the whole developing cycle, affecting variables, for example, crop yield, protection from vermin and infections, flexibility to natural circumstances, and the general progress of the gather. The choice cycle includes a mix of science, experience, and cautious thought of different variables that add to the ideal development of plants.

One of the essential contemplations while choosing seeds is the kind of yield or plant that the rancher means to develop. Various yields have unmistakable assortments, each with its own arrangement of qualities and necessities. For instance, assuming that a rancher is intending to develop tomatoes, they should look over assortments that suit their particular requirements, like determinate or vague sorts, cherry tomatoes, or bigger beefsteak tomatoes. Understanding the particular necessities and development propensities for the picked crop is fundamental for fruitful development.

The idea of open-pollinated, half breed, and hereditarily changed seeds likewise assumes a vital part in seed choice. Open-pollinated seeds are those pollinated by normal methods, like breeze, bugs, or birds. These seeds produce establishes that intently look like the parent plant, guaranteeing hereditary dependability. Then again, half and half seeds result from the purposeful cross-fertilization of two distinct however firmly related assortments to acquire explicit characteristics, like infection obstruction or expanded yield. Cross breed seeds frequently show heterosis or mixture life, prompting improved execution contrasted with their parent plants. Hereditarily changed (GM) seeds have gone through hereditary designing to present explicit attributes, like protection from vermin or resilience to herbicides. The decision between these seed types relies upon factors like the rancher's objectives, ecological contemplations, and administrative perspectives in their area.

Neighborhood transformation and environment strength are basic variables impacting seed choice. Seeds that have adjusted to the nearby environment, soil conditions, and other ecological elements are bound to flourish and deliver a fruitful reap. Ranchers should consider the temperature, precipitation examples, elevation, and other climatic components of their locale while choosing seeds. Environment versatile assortments are intended to endure outrageous weather patterns, giving a degree of soundness and protection from flighty environment changes.

Notwithstanding environment contemplations, soil quality and sythesis are vital in seed choice. Various yields have shifting soil inclinations, and choosing seeds that are appropriate to the particular soil states of the development region is fundamental for ideal development. Soil testing can give significant bits of knowledge into supplement levels, pH, and different variables that effect seed germination and plant improvement. Equipped with this data, ranchers can arrive at informed conclusions about which seeds are the most ideal for their specific soil conditions.

The length of the developing season is another significant variable impacting seed choice. A few yields have short developing seasons and can flourish in cooler environments, while others require longer times of warmth and daylight. Understanding the length of the developing season in a particular locale assists ranchers with picking seeds that can finish their lifecycle inside the accessible time span. This thought is particularly significant in regions with unmistakable seasons, where ice or outrageous temperatures might restrict the development time frame.

Protection from irritations and infections is a key characteristic that ranchers search for while choosing seeds. Certain harvest assortments have inherent protection from normal nuisances and sicknesses, lessening the requirement for compound mediations. This advantages the climate as well as adds to feasible and eco-accommodating cultivating rehearses. By picking seeds with normal obstruction qualities, ranchers can relieve the gamble of yield misfortune and limit the utilization of pesticides, encouraging a better and more adjusted environment.

Seed accessibility and access are functional contemplations that impact seed determination. Ranchers should evaluate the accessibility of the ideal seeds in their district and guarantee that they have dependable admittance to an adequate amount. The accessibility of value seeds from respectable sources adds to the outcome of the development adventure. Now and again, ranchers might select to store seeds for sometime later, requiring a comprehension of appropriate seed stockpiling practices to keep up with reasonability.

Neighborhood and customary information likewise assumes a huge part in seed choice. Native assortments that have been developed and adjusted to nearby circumstances over ages might offer remarkable benefits. Ranchers who tap into customary information frequently benefit from the insight of their progenitors, acquiring bits of knowledge into seed assortments that have endured everyday hardship. This information sharing adds to the conservation of biodiversity and the proceeded with progress of cultivating rehearses well established in the neighborhood culture.

Crop turn and enhancement procedures further effect seed choice. Ranchers rehearsing crop turn intend to break vermin and sickness cycles, further develop soil wellbeing, and upgrade by and large harvest yield. In such frameworks, the choice of seeds lines up with the rotational arrangement, guaranteeing that each harvest adds to the feasible administration of the rural biological system.

Expansion, including the development of various harvests, can likewise impact seed choice. Various harvests have different supplement necessities and development designs, and choosing integral seeds can improve generally speaking homestead efficiency.

In the period of present day horticulture, mechanical headways have presented accuracy cultivating methods that can impact seed determination. Remote detecting advancements, information investigation, and prescient demonstrating offer bits of knowledge into elements, for example, soil dampness levels, temperature varieties, and potential nuisance flare-ups. Ranchers outfitted with this data can settle on information driven choices while picking seeds, improving asset use and improving the probability of an effective reap.

As ranchers explore the mind boggling course of seed determination, they frequently look for direction from agrarian expansion administrations, agronomists, and individual ranchers. These sources give significant data on the presentation of various seed assortments in unambiguous areas, offering viable bits of knowledge in light of true encounters. The trading of information inside the cultivating local area establishes a cooperative climate where best practices are shared, and challenges are all in all tended to.

The job of seed organizations and reproducers in the seed choice cycle couldn't possibly be more significant. These substances put resources into innovative work to make better than ever seed assortments with helpful attributes. The coordinated effort among ranchers and seed organizations is a harmonious relationship, with ranchers giving input on seed execution, and organizations answering by refining and creating seed assortments that line up with the developing necessities of horticulture.

Seed quality is a non-debatable part of seed choice. Excellent seeds show attributes, for example, high germination rates, hereditary immaculateness, and life. Ranchers should focus on acquiring seeds from legitimate sources that stick to quality guidelines. Legitimate seed taking care of, stockpiling, and transportation likewise assume a significant part in keeping up with seed quality all through the production network. Quality confirmation rehearses add to the general achievement and supportability of horticultural undertakings.

Seed choice is definitely not a one-size-fits-all cycle; it is a progressing and dynamic part of cultivating that requires nonstop transformation. Ecological changes, market requests, and developing horticultural practices require an adaptable way to deal with seed choice. Ranchers who embrace development and remain informed about the most recent headways in horticulture are better prepared to pursue vital decisions that upgrade the flexibility and efficiency of their harvests.

All in all, the craftsmanship and study of choosing the right seeds for development include a nuanced comprehension of different variables that effect plant development. From environment and soil conditions to bug opposition and nearby information, every thought adds to the multifaceted woven artwork of fruitful cultivating. As ranchers explore the intricacies of seed determination, they become stewards of biodiversity, heroes of maintainability, and central members in the sensitive dance among nature and agribusiness. The right seeds, painstakingly picked and supported, hold the commitment of plentiful harvests and a maintainable future for a long time into the future.

2.3 Planting and germination process

The planting and germination process is an essential stage in the existence pattern of plants, denoting the start of their excursion from seed to develop plant. This interaction includes a progression of multifaceted advances that, when executed with care and consideration, set the establishment for solid development and improvement. Understanding the subtleties of planting and germination is fundamental for grounds-keepers, ranchers, and anybody participated in developing plants, as it straightforwardly impacts the outcome of the whole developing season.

The most important phase in the establishing system is choosing top notch seeds. The selection of seeds assumes a basic part in deciding the potential for a fruitful gather. Ranchers and landscapers should consider factors, for example, seed feasibility, germination rates, and the particular qualities of the ideal plant assortment. Seeds ought to be acquired from legitimate sources to guarantee their quality, and their determination ought to line up with the planned reason for development, whether for food creation, finishing, or different purposes.

Prior to planting, seeds might go through different medicines to improve their germination potential. Scarification, a cycle that includes scratching or scratching the seed coat, conquers torpidity in certain seeds. Separation, then again, mimics the regular cold time frame that specific seeds expect to break lethargy. These pre-establishing medicines mean to make ideal circumstances for germination and work on the general progress of the establishing system.

The decision of establishing strategy relies upon variables like the kind of plant, ecological circumstances, and the size of development. Direct cultivating includes setting seeds straightforwardly into the dirt where the plant will develop. This technique is normal for crops like beans, corn, and carrots. On the other hand, seeds can be begun inside or in controlled conditions through a cycle known as germination or seed beginning. This considers an early advantage on the developing season and is especially favorable in locales with more limited developing seasons.

Soil planning is a critical part of the establishing system. The dirt ought to be all around depleted, free, and wealthy in supplements to establish an ideal climate for seed germination.

Procedures like plowing and changing the dirt with natural matter add to its richness and construction. Moreover, understanding the pH necessities of the particular plants to be developed guarantees that the dirt gives an optimal developing medium.

The profundity at which seeds are established changes relying upon the sort of plant. Rules for establishing profundity are commonly given on seed parcels or in development guides. When in doubt, bigger seeds are planted further than more modest seeds. Legitimate establishing profundity is basic for guaranteeing that seeds get the perfect proportion of dampness, warmth, and oxygen for germination. Establishing too shallow or too profound can block the germination cycle.

Watering is a vital calculate the germination cycle. Seeds need dampness to mellow the seed coat and actuate proteins that start germination. Notwithstanding, overwatering can prompt issues like parasitic development or decay. The objective is to keep up with steady soil dampness without waterlogging. Watering procedures, for example, utilizing a fine fog or a delicate watering can, assist with forestalling soil unsettling influence and establish a climate helpful for germination.

Temperature is another basic component affecting seed germination. Various plants have explicit temperature necessities for ideal germination, frequently falling inside a scope of temperatures. Warm-season crops by and large require higher temperatures for germination than cool-season crops. Nursery workers can utilize strategies, for example, germination mats or ecological controls in indoor settings to keep up with the proper temperature for seed germination.

Light prerequisites during the germination cycle shift among plant species. While certain seeds expect openness to light for germination, others favor obscurity. Light-delicate seeds are ordinarily little and surface-planted, as they depend on light entrance for the commencement of germination. Conversely, bigger seeds that are covered in the dirt might develop all the more effectively in dimness. Understanding the light inclinations of explicit plants is fundamental for giving the right circumstances to germination.

Whenever seeds have been planted and the underlying prerequisites for germination have been met, the rise of the seedling marks the following stage in the vegetation's cycle. The main arrangement of leaves, known as cotyledons, rises out of the seed, furnishing the youthful plant with its underlying wellspring of energy through photosynthesis. As the seedling develops, it grows genuine leaves, which are particular from the cotyledons and look like the leaves of the experienced plant.

Seedlings are especially weak in their beginning phases, and mind should be taken to furnish them with ideal circumstances for development. Satisfactory dividing between seedlings forestalls stuffing, permitting each plant to get adequate light, supplements, and wind current. Diminishing might be important to eliminate abundance seedlings and advance the sound improvement of the excess plants.

Relocating is a typical practice where seedlings began inside or in controlled conditions are moved to their last developing areas. This interaction considers better control of the developing climate, security from unfriendly atmospheric conditions, and a lengthy developing season. Relocating ought to be done cautiously to limit weight on the seedlings, and it is normally coordinated to correspond with ideal outside developing circumstances.

The wellbeing and life of seedlings rely upon the accessibility of supplements in the dirt. Treatment is a critical part of the germination and early development stages. Applying a fair and fitting compost guarantees that seedlings get the fundamental supplements they need for vigorous turn of events. Natural revisions, like fertilizer, can likewise add to soil ripeness and give a consistent arrival of supplements.

Weeding is a continuous errand during the germination and seedling stages. Weeds rival arising plants for supplements, water, and daylight. Successful weed administration includes customary assessment of the establishing region, manual expulsion of weeds, or the utilization of mulch to stifle weed development. Keeping the developing climate free of contending vegetation upholds the sound development of sprouting seeds and youthful seedlings.

Assurance from vermin and illnesses is fundamental for shield the weak seedlings. Normal nuisances like aphids, caterpillars, and slugs can harm or obliterate youthful plants. Sicknesses, frequently brought about by growths or microorganisms, can spread quickly in favorable conditions. Incorporated bug the executives (IPM) works on, including the utilization of normal hunters, organic controls, and preventive measures, assist with moderating the dangers related with irritations and sicknesses.

Natural factors like breeze, temperature vacillations, and outrageous climate occasions can influence the germination and early development stages. Giving insurance through measures, for example, windbreaks, line covers, or shade material makes a more steady and good microclimate for youthful plants. Checking weather conditions conjectures and answering proactively to potential difficulties add to the flexibility of sprouting seeds and seedlings.

The germination and early development stages are basic periods in the existence pattern of plants, setting the direction for future turn of events. Legitimate consideration, thoughtfulness regarding ecological circumstances, and convenient intercessions add to the progress of this basic stage. As seedlings mature and create, they change from the weakness of germination to the power of laid out plants, prepared to confront the difficulties of the developing season.

All in all, the planting and germination process address a pivotal crossroads in the lifecycle of plants, where cautious meticulousness and adherence to best practices lay the foundation for fruitful development. From the choice of great seeds to the sustaining of arising seedlings, each step adds to the general wellbeing and efficiency of the plant. As nursery workers, ranchers, and cultivators leave on the excursion from seed to develop plant, a profound comprehension of the complexities of the germination cycle turns into the foundation of a plentiful gather and the acknowledgment of the likely inborn in each seed.

2.4 Tips for successful seedling development

The effective improvement of seedlings is a basic stage in the development pattern of plants, as it lays the preparation for hearty and solid plants in the later phases of development. Whether you are a home nursery worker, rancher, or horticulturist, understanding the critical tips for fruitful seedling improvement is fundamental for upgrading plant development, guaranteeing exceptional returns, and encouraging by and large plant wellbeing.

Begin with Top notch Seeds:

The underpinning of effective seedling advancement starts with the choice of great seeds. Choose seeds from legitimate providers or believed sources, guaranteeing they are new, practical, and liberated from sickness. The intrinsic hereditary capability of the seed straightforwardly impacts the force and versatility of the subsequent seedlings.

Give Ideal Developing Medium:

The developing medium, or seed-beginning blend, is significant for seedling improvement. It ought to be well-depleting, lightweight, and sterile to forestall sicknesses. Consider utilizing a blend explicitly intended for seed beginning, or make a custom mix with parts like peat greenery, vermiculite, and perlite. This gives a reasonable climate that energizes solid root improvement.

Utilize Clean Holders:

Whether you pick plastic plate, biodegradable pots, or different holders for beginning your seeds, tidiness is critical. Sanitize holders before use to dispose of any potential microbes that could hurt the seedlings. This safeguard measure establishes a climate helpful for ideal seedling development.

Appropriate Planting Profundity:

Sowing seeds at the right profundity is significant for effective germination and seedling advancement. Observe the rules gave on seed parcels, as various plants have fluctuating profundity necessities. Establishing too shallow or too profound can influence the development of seedlings and their resulting development.

Give Sufficient Light:

Sufficient light is fundamental for sound seedling advancement. In the case of beginning seeds inside, place plate close to a south-bound window or utilize fake lighting frameworks, for example, fluorescent or Drove develop lights. Guarantee that light is steady, and position lights at the legitimate separation from seedlings to forestall leggy development.

Keep up with Ideal Temperature:

Seed germination and early seedling development are temperature-touchy cycles. Most seeds grow well inside unambiguous temperature ranges, so giving ideal conditions is fundamental. Utilize a seedling heat mat to keep up with predictable temperatures, particularly for warm-season crops, or think about a controlled climate for more exact temperature the executives.

Watering Reliably:

Legitimate watering is a basic calculate seedling improvement. Seedlings are delicate to both overwatering and underwatering. Keep the developing medium reliably damp however not waterlogged. Water seedlings from the base when conceivable to empower solid root advancement. Utilize a delicate splash or watering can to try not to upset the fragile seedlings.

Diminishing Seedlings:

Whenever seedlings have arisen, diminishing is important to give satisfactory room to the leftover plants to develop. Stuffed seedlings vie for supplements, light, and space, prompting frail and leggy development. Eliminate abundance seedlings, leaving simply the best and most powerful people.

Prepare Suitably:

While seedlings at first depend on the supplements put away in the seed, they ultimately need supplemental preparation. Begin with a half-strength, adjusted fluid manure when the main arrangement of genuine leaves shows up. Change the recurrence and fixation in light of the particular necessities of the plants and the proposals on the compost bundle.

Solidify Off Seedlings:

Prior to relocating seedlings into the outside nursery or field, it's urgent to solidify them off. This includes slowly presenting them to open air conditions, like daylight, wind, and fluctuating temperatures. Start with brief lengths and slowly increment openness to help seedlings adjust and keep away from shock.

Timing is Vital:

Seedlings have explicit development necessities, including day length and temperature, which change among plant species.

Think about the best timing for beginning seeds inside or straightforwardly planting them outside in light of the nearby environment and the plant's particular requirements. Beginning too soon or past the point of no return can affect the progress of seedling advancement.

Safeguard from Vermin:

Seedlings are powerless against vermin like aphids, thrips, and insect parasites. Routinely investigate seedlings for indications of bug invasion, and go to preventive lengths, for example, presenting advantageous bugs or utilizing regular cures like neem oil. A sound and peaceful climate adds to hearty seedling improvement.

Energize Air Course:

Legitimate air course is significant for forestalling issues like damping-off (a parasitic illness that influences seedlings) and advancing in general plant wellbeing. Use fans or give sufficient separating between seedlings to guarantee great air development. Abstain from congestion and inordinate stickiness, which can make conditions ideal for contagious infections.

Screen for Sicknesses:

Seedlings can be defenseless to different sicknesses, especially parasitic diseases. Watch out for the general strength of the seedlings, and expeditiously address any indications of illness, like staining, shrinking, or uncommon development. Appropriate sterilization, well-depleting soil, and great air dissemination add to illness counteraction.

Be Aware of Supplement Needs:

As seedlings develop, their supplement needs advance. Change preparation rehearses in view of the formative phase of the seedlings. Change to a fair, original capacity manure as the seedlings mature and plan for transplantation. Think about involving natural manures for a gradual arrival of supplements.

Consider Friend Planting:

Buddy planting includes decisively setting plants in nearness to each other to improve development and hinder bothers. Understanding the similarity of various plant species and consolidating buddy establishing standards can add to a better developing climate for seedlings.

Put resources into Quality Soil Alterations:

Improve the supplement content and design of the developing medium by consolidating quality soil corrections. Natural matter, like fertilizer, very much spoiled compost, or worm castings, further develops soil ripeness and gives a supplement rich climate to seedling improvement. Revisions likewise add to more readily water maintenance and seepage.

Mulch for Dampness Maintenance:

Applying a layer of natural mulch around seedlings holds soil dampness, manage temperature, and smother weed development. Mulching is especially useful for open air seedlings, as it makes a defensive layer that upholds sound root improvement and decreases water pressure.

Change Light Force:

As seedlings develop, changing the light force becomes significant. Raise or lower counterfeit lights to keep the ideal separation between the light source and the seedlings. Guaranteeing that light force stays fitting as seedlings create forestalls issues like extending or hindered development.

Notice and Answer Quickly:

Normal perception is vital to fruitful seedling improvement. Screen seedlings for any indications of stress, supplement lacks, or nuisance related issues. Expeditiously answer any difficulties by changing ecological circumstances, tending to supplement uneven characters, or carrying out bug control measures. Proactive administration adds to in general seedling wellbeing.

Pick Suitable Holders:

If beginning seeds in holders, pick proper estimated compartments with great waste. This takes into consideration sound root advancement and forestalls waterlogged circumstances. Consider utilizing biodegradable pots that can be planted straightforwardly into the dirt, limiting transfer shock during the progress to outside conditions.

Abstain from Congestion:

Stuffing seedlings, whether in plate or establishing beds, upsets their admittance to light, air, and supplements. Satisfactory dividing is fundamental for forestalling rivalry and guaranteeing that every seedling gets the assets it needs for ideal turn of events. Keep suggested dividing rules for the particular plants being developed.

Carry out Progression Planting:

Progression planting includes stunning establishing times to guarantee a consistent collect all through the developing season. This approach expands the utilization of accessible space and assets while forestalling an excess of produce at one time. Progression planting is particularly valuable for crops with a short collect window.

Practice Great Cleanliness:

Keeping up with great cleanliness works on during the seedling improvement stage adds to a sound developing climate. Clean instruments, plate, and compartments between utilizations to forestall the spread of infections. Discard any plant trash appropriately, and abstain from acquainting microorganisms with the developing region.

Remain Informed and Adjust:

Remain educated about the particular requirements regarding the plants you are developing and be ready to adjust your practices in view of the exceptional attributes of every species. Cultivating and cultivating are dynamic undertakings, and being responsive to the advancing necessities of your seedlings improves your capacity to encourage effective turn of events.

Chapter 3

Cultivating Jackfruit: Nurturing Growth

In the tremendous spread of farming scenes, where the sun kisses the earth and the dirt murmurs mysteries of fruitfulness, one can find a novel and strong tree standing tall — the jackfruit tree. The jackfruit, experimentally known as Artocarpus heterophyllus, is a tropical tree natural product local to southwest India. Venerated for its monstrous size, flexibility, and dietary benefit, the jackfruit has turned into an image of food and strength in many regions of the planet.

As farming practices develop and social orders wrestle with the difficulties of food security, the jackfruit arises as an encouraging sign — a demonstration of the force of nature and human inventiveness. Developing jackfruit includes something other than sowing a seed; it requires a profound comprehension of the tree's science, ecological circumstances, and the many-sided dance among people and their normal environmental factors.

The excursion of developing jackfruit starts with the choice of the right assortment. Jackfruit trees display critical hereditary variety, with different cultivars appropriate for various environments and soil types. Ranchers and horticulturists cautiously pick the assortment that lines up with their area's circumstances, taking into account factors like temperature, precipitation, and height. This insightful determination makes way for a fruitful development adventure.

When the assortment is picked, the following significant step is spread. Jackfruit trees can be engendered through seeds or vegetative techniques like uniting and sprouting. While seeds are promptly accessible from the full grown natural product, vegetative engendering guarantees the maintenance of positive characteristics and speeds up the tree's development. Gifted hands cautiously unite scions onto rootstocks, guaranteeing an association that will lead to a hearty and productive tree.

As the jackfruit tree flourishes and starts its excursion upward, consideration goes to soil planning. Jackfruit trees flourish in very much depleted, loamy soil wealthy in natural matter. Ranchers utilize different strategies, including treating the soil and cover trimming, to improve soil ripeness and design. The wellbeing of the dirt straightforwardly impacts the tree's capacity to ingest supplements, lay out major areas of strength for a framework, and oppose sicknesses.

Pair with soil planning, water the executives turns into a basic part of jackfruit development. The tree's water necessities change at various phases of development, with youthful saplings requiring more incessant water system than mature trees. Feasible water rehearses, for example, water reaping and dribble water system, ration this valuable asset as well as add to the general soundness of the environment.

The jackfruit tree, with its gleaming green leaves and solid branches, isn't just a farming ware; it is a green partner in the battle against environmental change. The tree's enormous shelter gives conceal, diminishing ground temperatures and alleviating the effect of heatwaves. Besides, the jackfruit tree is a hero in carbon sequestration, locking away air carbon dioxide and adding to the worldwide work to battle environmental change.

As the tree develops, it starts to prove to be fruitful, and the plantation changes into a dynamic embroidery of hanging jackfruits. The natural product, frequently alluded to as the world's biggest tree-borne organic product, can arrive at sizes of as much as 80 pounds. A solitary tree can possibly yield many pounds of jackfruit every year, offering a plentiful reap for the constant cultivator.

The jackfruit's culinary flexibility adds to its charm. The ready, sweet arils are a tropical pleasure, delighted in new or integrated into a bunch of dishes. From curries and stews to pastries and smoothies, the jackfruit's delicious tissue fits a wide cluster of culinary manifestations. In its unripe, green state, jackfruit turns into an exquisite substitute for meat, finding a spot in veggie lover and vegetarian eats less all over the planet.

Past its culinary purposes, the jackfruit has earned consideration for its nourishing profile. Plentiful in dietary fiber, nutrients, and minerals, the organic product offers a restorative expansion to different eating regimens.

Additionally, progressing research investigates the possible restorative properties of different jackfruit parts, opening new roads for saddling the tree's advantages in the domain of medical services.

In the multifaceted dance of development, vermin and sickness the executives arises as a sensitive accomplice. Jackfruit trees, similar to some other yield, face dangers from bugs, growths, and microscopic organisms. Coordinated bug the executives methodologies, joining natural, social, and compound controls, assist with finding some kind of harmony between safeguarding the harvest and saving the climate. Careful checking and early intercession guarantee that the jackfruit plantation stays versatile against possible dangers.

The excursion of developing jackfruit isn't without its difficulties. Environment changeability, flighty weather conditions, and changing ecological circumstances present huge obstacles for ranchers. Accordingly, supportable and environment shrewd practices come to the very front. Agroforestry, intercropping, and permaculture standards are embraced to make strong biological systems that cradle against the effects of environmental change.

The social and monetary components of jackfruit development weave an embroidery of interconnectedness. In numerous areas, jackfruit development is profoundly implanted in the social texture, molding customs and vocations. Smallholder ranchers, with their hands in the dirt and hearts in the plantation, assume a significant part in supporting this agroecosystem. As overseers of biodiversity and stewards of the land, they typify the soul of developing jackfruit.

Market elements likewise assume a significant part in the development story. The rising worldwide interest for supportable and plant-based food choices has situated jackfruit as a headliner in the culinary world. Business people and agribusinesses immediately jump all over the chance, making esteem added items and laying out jackfruit as a product with financial potential. From jackfruit chips to canned jackfruit in saline solution, the market differentiates, offering purchasers new and imaginative ways of encountering this tropical fortune.

Notwithstanding, the excursion of developing jackfruit reaches out past the limits of the plantation and the market. It interlaces with more extensive issues of food security, natural preservation, and local area strength. The maintainable development of jackfruit isn't just about procuring a collect; it is tied in with encouraging an agreeable connection among people and the land, among horticulture and nature.

In the journey for supportable farming, agroecology arises as a directing way of thinking. Established in biological standards, agroecology looks to fit horticultural frameworks with the regular habitat, advancing biodiversity, soil wellbeing, and strength. The development of jackfruit adjusts consistently with the fundamentals of agroecology, delineating how a tree can be in excess of a wellspring of organic product — it tends to be a watchman of environmental equilibrium.

The development of jackfruit entices us to consider our relationship with food and the land. In this present reality where monoculture and modern horticulture frequently rule the story, the jackfruit remains as a contradiction — an update that variety is the heartbeat of flexibility. The plantation, with its bunch shades and surfaces, typifies the wealth of agrobiodiversity, welcoming us to reconsider a future where farming supports both the body and the planet.

As the jackfruit tree proceeds to develop and prove to be fruitful, it welcomes us to think about the interconnectedness of every living thing. The roots that anchor it to the earth are an illustration for the profound associations between soil, water, and life. The branches that stretch towards the sky represent the goals for a manageable and regenerative future. In the shade of the jackfruit tree, networks accumulate, stories are shared, and a feeling of having a place blooms — a demonstration of the social texture woven by the development of this noteworthy tree.

The excursion of developing jackfruit is an excursion of sustaining development — of trees, of networks, and of the aggregate human soul. An excursion rises above the limits of fields and plantations, venturing into the domains of culture, supportability, and flexibility. As we develop jackfruit, we develop a dream of an existence where farming is a regenerative power, where the land flourishes, and where the our rewards for so much hard work support ages to come.

In the calm stir of leaves and the unpretentious fragrance of maturing organic product, the tale of developing jackfruit unfurls — an account of trust, of food, and of the significant association among people and the earth. In the core of the plantation, where the sun-dappled ground supports fallen jackfruits, the pattern of development keeps, repeating the immortal mood of nature. Developing jackfruit isn't simply a farming practice; it is a hit the dance floor with the components, an amicable song that reverberates through the patterns of life.

3.1 Ideal climate and soil conditions for Jackfruit cultivation

In the perplexing embroidery of horticultural scenes, the development of jackfruit remains as a demonstration of the exchange between nature's subtleties and human resourcefulness. To leave on an effective excursion of jackfruit development, understanding the ideal environment and soil conditions becomes fundamental. The jackfruit tree, with its starting points in the rainforests of southwest India, has adjusted to a heat and humidity. In that capacity, it flourishes in locales described by unambiguous temperature ranges, precipitation levels, and soil attributes.

The main thought in developing jackfruit is the environment. Jackfruit trees are intrinsically tropical, requiring warm temperatures to prosper. The ideal temperature range for jackfruit development falls between 20 to 30 degrees Celsius (68 to 86 degrees Fahrenheit).

While the tree can endure brief temperature decreases, delayed openness to temperatures under 0 degrees Celsius (32 degrees Fahrenheit) can be negative. Ice is a huge danger to jackfruit trees, and regions inclined to ice may not give an ideal environment to fruitful development.

Precipitation assumes a significant part in the development and improvement of jackfruit trees. They flourish in locales with a particular wet and dry season, getting a yearly precipitation of roughly 1000 to 3000 millimeters. Satisfactory water accessibility during the developing season is fundamental for the tree's foundation, blossoming, and fruiting. Notwithstanding, over the top precipitation, particularly during the blossoming time frame, can prompt unfortunate organic product set and expanded powerlessness to illnesses.

Daylight is one more key part of the best environment for jackfruit development. The tree requires adequate daylight for photosynthesis and by and large development. An area that gets full sun openness, with no less than 6 to 8 hours of direct daylight day to day, is great for the ideal improvement of jackfruit trees. Deficient daylight can bring about hindered development and diminished organic product creation.

Elevation is a component that impacts temperature and, thusly, the reasonableness of an area for jackfruit development. Jackfruit trees are for the most part developed at elevations going from ocean level to around 1500 meters. Past this reach, temperature varieties might influence the tree's development and fruiting examples. Thusly, choosing an area inside the predetermined height territory adds to the general progress of jackfruit development.

While the environment makes way for jackfruit development, soil conditions structure the establishment whereupon the tree lays out its foundations and draws fundamental supplements. Jackfruit trees are versatile to an assortment of soil types, yet they flourish best in very much depleted, loamy soils wealthy in natural matter. The dirt ought to have a somewhat acidic to nonpartisan pH, going from 6.0 to 7.5. This pH range is helpful for the take-up of supplements and supports the general strength of the tree.

Soil surface is one more basic part of jackfruit development. Loamy soils, portrayed by a decent combination of sand, residue, and earth, give an optimal medium to root improvement. The very much depleted nature of loamy soils forestalls waterlogging, which is inconvenient to the tree's underground root growth. Satisfactory waste guarantees that oxygen arrives at the roots, advancing solid development.

In locales with heavier dirt soils, consolidating natural matter through treating the soil or cover trimming can improve soil design and fruitfulness. Alternately, in sandy soils, the expansion of natural matter further develops water maintenance and supplement accessibility. Soil corrections assume a crucial part in establishing a climate that upholds the supplement needs of the jackfruit tree all through its life cycle.

Besides, the jackfruit tree is delicate to waterlogging, which can prompt root decay and different illnesses. In this way, choosing a site with very much depleted soil is critical for the fruitful development of jackfruit. Carrying out appropriate water the board rehearses, for example, shape furrowing and the utilization of raised beds, mitigates the gamble of waterlogging and guarantees the strength of the tree.

Notwithstanding soil surface and waste, the presence of adequate natural matter in the dirt is fundamental for jackfruit development. Natural matter upgrades soil richness, water maintenance, and microbial movement. Ranchers frequently integrate very much decayed fertilizer or natural compost into the dirt to work on its natural substance. This training gives fundamental supplements to the tree as well as advances a sound soil environment.

While the ideal environment and soil conditions give a structure to fruitful jackfruit development, recognizing the flexibility of the tree is significant. Jackfruit trees have been known to flourish in assorted conditions, exhibiting their flexibility to fluctuating circumstances. Be that as it may, upgrading the environment and soil boundaries improves the tree's power, efficiency, and protection from bugs and illnesses.

In locales where the normal environment and soil conditions go amiss from the ideal, ranchers utilize different strategies to make microenvironments that favor jackfruit development. This might incorporate the utilization of windbreaks to safeguard major areas of strength for against, the production of shade designs to moderate exorbitant daylight, and the execution of water the board frameworks to address varieties in precipitation.

Environment savvy agribusiness rehearses additionally become possibly the most important factor, adjusting jackfruit development to supportable and strong cultivating approaches. Agroforestry, for example, coordinates jackfruit trees with different yields, cultivating biodiversity and making a synergistic connection between various components of the agroecosystem. This not just improves the general strength of the ranch yet in addition adds to environmental equilibrium.

All in all, the development of jackfruit is an amicable cooperation between the tree, the environment, and the dirt. The ideal environment for jackfruit development embraces tropical circumstances, with warm temperatures, unmistakable wet and dry seasons, and more than adequate daylight. Height, precipitation, and the evasion of ice are key contemplations in choosing a reasonable area for jackfruit plantations.

Similarly significant is the dirt, with very much depleted loamy soils giving an ideal medium to root improvement. A marginally acidic to impartial pH, combined with the fuse of natural matter, establishes a prolific climate that upholds the nourishing necessities of the jackfruit tree.

Thoughtfulness regarding soil surface, waste, and water the board further adds to the outcome of jackfruit development.

As farming countenances the difficulties of a changing environment and developing interest for manageable practices, the development of harvests like jackfruit becomes a science as well as a craftsmanship — a fragile hit the dance floor with nature. By getting it and regarding the ideal environment and soil conditions for jackfruit development, ranchers and cultivators can open the tree's maximum capacity, encouraging a relationship that supports both the land and its overseers. In the lavish plantations where jackfruit trees aim high, a story unfurls — an account of flexibility, versatility, and the persevering through association among mankind and the earth.

3.2 Choosing the right location for planting

In the perplexing trap of rural choices, one of the basic determinants of achievement is picking the right area for planting. Whether one is setting out on the development of harvests, plantations, or trees like the flexible jackfruit, the determination of an ideal site establishes the groundwork for a prospering farming undertaking. The cycle includes a nuanced comprehension of natural variables, microclimates, and the particular requirements of the picked plant. On account of jackfruit, a tree local to tropical districts, the significance of a reasonable area couldn't possibly be more significant.

The primary thought in picking the right area for establishing jackfruit is grasping the tree's regular living space and climatic inclinations. Jackfruit, with its beginnings in the rainforests of southwest India, is innately adjusted to a heat and humidity. It flourishes in areas described by warm temperatures, particular wet and dry seasons, and adequate daylight. Thusly, choosing an area that repeats these circumstances gives an early advantage to fruitful jackfruit development.

Temperature assumes a urgent part in the development and improvement of jackfruit trees. While they can endure a scope of temperatures, the ideal reach for ideal development falls between 20 to 30 degrees Celsius (68 to 86 degrees Fahrenheit). Ice is a critical danger to jackfruit trees, and regions inclined to ice may not be reasonable for development. Thusly, picking an area with an environment that lines up with the temperature inclinations of jackfruit guarantees the tree's capacity to flourish and prove to be fruitful.

Height is another component that impacts temperature and, subsequently, the reasonableness of an area for jackfruit development. Jackfruit trees are by and large developed at heights going from ocean level to around 1500 meters. Past this reach, temperature varieties might affect the tree's development and fruiting examples. In this manner, choosing an area inside the predefined elevation range adds to the general progress of jackfruit development.

Notwithstanding temperature contemplations, precipitation designs are urgent in deciding the right area for establishing jackfruit. The tree flourishes in locales with a particular wet and dry season, getting a yearly precipitation of roughly 1000 to 3000 millimeters. Sufficient water accessibility during the developing season is fundamental for the tree's foundation, blossoming, and fruiting. Consequently, districts with distinct stormy and dry periods are great for effective jackfruit development.

Daylight, a crucial part of plant development, is a key thought while picking an area for jackfruit planting. The tree requires adequate daylight for photosynthesis and generally improvement. An area that gets full sun openness, with no less than 6 to 8 hours of direct daylight day to day, is great for the ideal development of jackfruit trees. Lacking daylight can bring about hindered development and decreased natural product creation.

Past climatic elements, the actual qualities of the dirt assume a vital part in deciding the reasonableness of an area for jackfruit development. Jackfruit trees are versatile to an assortment of soil types, however they flourish best in very much depleted, loamy soils wealthy in natural matter. The dirt ought to have a marginally acidic to nonpartisan pH, going from 6.0 to 7.5. This pH range is helpful for the take-up of supplements and supports the general wellbeing of the tree.

Soil surface is one more basic part of jackfruit development. Loamy soils, described by a decent combination of sand, residue, and mud, give an optimal medium to root improvement. The all around depleted nature of loamy soils forestalls waterlogging, which is negative to the tree's underground root growth. Satisfactory seepage guarantees that oxygen arrives at the roots, advancing solid development.

In districts with heavier earth soils, consolidating natural matter through fertilizing the soil or cover trimming can upgrade soil construction and ripeness. On the other hand, in sandy soils, the expansion of natural matter further develops water maintenance and supplement accessibility. Soil changes assume an imperative part in establishing a climate that upholds the supplement needs of the jackfruit tree all through its life cycle.

Water the executives is one more pivotal viewpoint to consider while picking the right area for jackfruit planting. The tree is delicate to waterlogging, which can prompt root decay and different illnesses. In this manner, choosing a site with very much depleted soil is central for effective jackfruit development. Carrying out legitimate water the executives rehearses, for example, shape furrowing and the utilization of raised beds, mitigates the gamble of waterlogging and guarantees the wellbeing of the tree.

Wind openness is an element that ought not be disregarded, particularly in that frame of mind areas of strength for to. Jackfruit trees have a shallow root foundation, and extreme breeze can represent a gamble of evacuating or harming the trees.

Establishing windbreaks or choosing areas protected areas of strength for from adds to the soundness and in general prosperity of jackfruit plantations.

Past these ecological contemplations, the closeness to different harvests and the potential for intercropping can impact the choice on the area for jackfruit planting. Agroforestry rehearses, which coordinate trees like jackfruit with different harvests, add to biodiversity and make a synergistic relationship inside the rural biological system. Buddy planting with viable yields can improve generally speaking efficiency and maintainability.

The financial part of picking an establishing area likewise assumes a huge part. In numerous districts, jackfruit development is profoundly implanted in the social texture, and smallholder ranchers are the overseers of this practice. Supporting nearby networks and guaranteeing evenhanded admittance to land add to the feasible and moral development of jackfruit.

All in all, the most common way of picking the right area for establishing jackfruit includes an extensive comprehension of climatic circumstances, soil qualities, and ecological variables. The tree's tropical beginnings and explicit environment inclinations make it significant to choose an area that lines up with its temperature, precipitation, and daylight necessities. The actual properties of the dirt, including surface, waste, and supplement content, further impact the tree's development and efficiency.

Water the board rehearses, wind openness, and the potential for intercropping add to the general reasonableness of an area for jackfruit development. As horticulture keeps on developing despite environmental change and developing requests for feasible practices, the choice on where to establish jackfruit becomes a strategic decision as well as a guarantee to orchestrating with nature. In the painstakingly picked places where jackfruit trees flourish, a story unfurls — an account of versatility, flexibility, and the persevering through association between the earth and the people who support it.

3.3 Pruning and care for healthy tree development

In the craftsmanship and study of developing trees, scarcely any practices are all around as fundamental and groundbreaking as pruning. Pruning is a plant strategy that includes the particular evacuation of explicit pieces of a tree, like branches, buds, or roots. When applied with information and accuracy, pruning adds to sound tree advancement, further developed natural product creation, and generally speaking plantation the board. With regards to jackfruit development, a tree known for its strong development and huge fruiting, the meaning of legitimate pruning couldn't possibly be more significant.

The objectives of pruning in jackfruit development are multi-layered. They envelop molding the tree for ideal development, dealing with its size, advancing daylight infiltration, and improving air course.

Moreover, pruning effectively eliminates sick or dead wood, diminishing the gamble of irritations and illnesses. The timing, methods, and recurrence of pruning fluctuate all through the tree's life cycle, requesting a nuanced come closer from cultivators.

Youthful jackfruit trees require developmental pruning to lay out a very much organized system for future development. This early mediation impacts the tree's shape, branch dispersion, and in general design. Normally acted in the initial not many years subsequent to planting, developmental pruning includes choosing a focal pioneer — a prevailing, upstanding stem that turns into the principal trunk. The expulsion of contending pioneers guarantees areas of strength for an even focal construction.

Branches that develop excessively near the ground are frequently pruned to make a reasonable trunk, advancing air flow and decreasing the gamble of parasitic illnesses. The expulsion of crossing or internal developing branches forestalls future primary issues and supports an open overhang. As the youthful jackfruit tree lays out its shape, developmental pruning makes way for a useful and reasonable mature tree.

As the tree develops, routine upkeep pruning turns into a fundamental part of care. This incorporates the expulsion of dead, sick, or harmed wood — a training known as "cleaning cuts." Deadwood fills in as a possible natural surroundings for bugs and microbes, and its convenient evacuation mitigates these dangers. Normal investigations likewise permit cultivators to immediately recognize and address any indications of infection or invasion.

Diminishing cuts, one more sort of support pruning, include the particular expulsion of branches to work on light entrance and air course inside the covering. Diminishing cuts decrease the thickness of the tree's foliage, forestalling the improvement of a thick and concealed inside. Sufficient daylight openness is critical for photosynthesis, organic product improvement, and the general wellbeing of the jackfruit tree.

Notwithstanding standard upkeep pruning, jackfruit trees benefit from revival pruning. This includes the expulsion of more seasoned, ineffective wood to animate new development and keep up with the tree's power. Revival pruning is especially important in more established plantations or dismissed trees, where the recharging of branches and foliage adds to supported efficiency.

Natural product diminishing, albeit not a conventional type of pruning, is a significant part of overseeing organic product load and advancing sound turn of events. Jackfruit trees are productive conveyors, frequently delivering countless natural products.

Nonetheless, to guarantee the ideal development and size of individual organic products, it is normal practice to thin the harvest. Diminishing includes specifically eliminating a portion of the creating natural products, permitting the excess ones to get more supplements and develop to their maximum capacity.

Pruning strategies change in light of the particular necessities of jackfruit trees. Heading cuts, where the terminal part of a branch is taken out, invigorate expanding and advance a bushier development propensity. Heading cuts are many times utilized in developmental pruning to shape the youthful tree. Then again, diminishing cuts include the evacuation of a whole branch or stem at its starting place. Diminishing cuts are instrumental in lessening thickness, working on light entrance, and overseeing generally speaking covering structure.

Crown decrease is a pruning method utilized to diminish the general size of the tree's covering. Here the tree has grown out of its dispensed space or to address likely perils. Crown decrease includes specifically eliminating branches to diminish the level and spread of the overhang while keeping up with the tree's regular structure. Cautious thought of branch design and development designs is critical to accomplishing a fair and tastefully satisfying outcome.

Pruning is certainly not a one-size-fits-all training, and its prosperity depends on a profound comprehension of the tree's science and development propensities. The planning of pruning is a basic component, and jackfruit trees are many times pruned during the torpid season — normally in the colder time of year or late-winter. Pruning during lethargy limits weight on the tree and lessens the gamble of infection transmission through fresh injuries.

The apparatuses utilized for pruning are similarly significant. Sharp, clean pruning apparatuses guarantee exact slices and limit harm to the tree. Pruning shears, loppers, and saws are normal apparatuses utilized in the different kinds of pruning cuts. Sanitizing instruments between cuts, particularly while moving between trees, forestalls the spread of sicknesses.

While pruning is a useful asset for molding tree development and advancing wellbeing, finding some kind of harmony is significant. Exorbitant pruning can prompt pressure, diminished development, and expanded weakness to nuisances and sicknesses. A prudent methodology, directed by a comprehension of the tree's regular structure and development propensities, guarantees that pruning improves instead of blocks the tree's prosperity.

As well as pruning, other consideration rehearses add to the general wellbeing and improvement of jackfruit trees. Satisfactory water system is pivotal, particularly during dry periods, to help the tree's water needs. Mulching around the foundation of the tree assists monitor with ruining dampness, stifle weeds, and direct soil temperature. Treatment, custom fitted to the particular supplement prerequisites of jackfruit, guarantees ideal development and natural product creation.

Vermin and illness the executives is a continuous part of tree care. Customary checking for indications of vermin or infections takes into consideration convenient mediation. Regular hunters, like advantageous bugs, can be urged to assist with controlling vermin populaces. Natural and incorporated bug the executives techniques limit the utilization of substance intercessions, lining up with maintainable and harmless to the ecosystem rehearses.

Past the specialized parts of pruning and care, the prosperity of jackfruit trees is unpredictably connected to the encompassing biological system. Agroecological standards, which accentuate the reliance of farming and biology, highlight the significance of developing trees as one with the climate. Agroforestry rehearses incorporate trees into assorted farming frameworks, encouraging biodiversity and environmental flexibility.

The social and financial components of tree care are similarly huge. In numerous districts, jackfruit development is profoundly implanted in social customs, giving food as well as a feeling of character and local area. Smallholder ranchers, with their generational information and active experience, assume a significant part in supporting and saving these horticultural heritages.

Taking everything into account, pruning and care are basic parts of the comprehensive way to deal with developing solid and useful jackfruit trees. From developmental pruning that shapes the youthful tree's design to routine upkeep pruning that tends to deadwood and advances air flow, each cut is an intentional activity with significant ramifications for the tree's prosperity. Natural product diminishing, revival pruning, and crown decrease further add to the general administration of the tree.

Pruning, when drawn nearer with information, expertise, and a profound comprehension of the tree's science, turns into a hit the dance floor with nature — a cooperation that sustains sound development and plentiful fruiting. Past the specialized viewpoints, the consideration of jackfruit trees encapsulates a more extensive obligation to manageable and regenerative farming. In the plantations where pruners move with reason among the branches, a story unfurls — an account of flexibility, stewardship, and the persevering through association among people and the trees they develop.

3.4 Dealing with common pests and diseases

In the unpredictable dance of horticulture, the fight against bugs and illnesses is a consistently present test. Jackfruit, a tree known for its flexibility and flexibility, isn't excluded from the dangers presented by bugs, organisms, and microbes. Powerful irritation and illness the executives are urgent for guaranteeing the wellbeing and efficiency of jackfruit plantations. Understanding the normal irritations and infections that burden jackfruit trees, alongside executing preventive and corrective measures, is a foundation of fruitful development.

One of the essential foes of jackfruit development is the jackfruit drill (Bactrocera dorsalis). This organic product fly lays its eggs on the outer layer of the natural product, and the subsequent hatchlings tunnel into the tissue, causing harm and working with the section of optional microbes. To oversee jackfruit drills, a mix of social and synthetic control measures is frequently utilized.

Social practices incorporate the evacuation and obliteration of swarmed natural products to break the existence pattern of the nuisance. Great plantation disinfection, like the brief assortment and removal of fallen natural products, decreases the probability of invasion. Moreover, the utilization of pheromone traps can help screen and control the number of inhabitants in grown-up natural product flies, disturbing their mating examples and decreasing egg-laying.

Compound control includes the use of insect sprays at explicit stretches during the fruiting season. The selection of insect sprays ought to be directed by contemplations like viability, ecological effect, and adherence to incorporated bug the executives (IPM) standards. Ranchers frequently pivot the utilization of various synthetic mixtures to limit the gamble of bugs creating opposition.

Another normal vermin influencing jackfruit is the mealybug (Planococcus citri). Mealybugs are sap-sucking bugs that overrun the leaves, stems, and product of jackfruit trees. Their presence can prompt hindered development, shriveling, and a decrease in natural product quality. Coordinated bother the executives techniques for mealybugs incorporate the presentation of normal hunters, for example, ladybugs and parasitic wasps, which assist with holding mealybug populaces under wraps.

Neem-based plans, known for their insecticidal properties, are likewise used as a biopesticide against mealybugs. Neem oil upsets the bug's life cycle and fills in as an obstacle for taking care of and egg-laying. Furthermore, green oils and insecticidal cleansers are utilized as elective control strategies that limit the effect on useful bugs and the climate.

In the domain of parasitic sicknesses, anthracnose (Colletotrichum gloeosporioides) represents a critical danger to jackfruit development. Anthracnose appears as dull sores on leaves, stems, and organic product, prompting untimely natural product drop and diminished attractiveness. The growth flourishes in warm and moist circumstances, making preventive measures significant for sickness the executives.

Social practices like pruning to further develop air flow, the expulsion of tainted plant material, and keeping up with appropriate dividing between trees add to anthracnose control. Fungicides containing copper compounds are regularly utilized in traditional horticulture to oversee anthracnose. Notwithstanding, natural other options, for example, biofungicides and neem-based definitions, offer harmless to the ecosystem choices for infectious prevention.

Fine buildup (Oidium spp.) is another parasitic infection that can influence jackfruit trees. This sickness presents as a white fine substance on leaves, repressing photosynthesis and compromising the tree's general wellbeing. Fine buildup flourishes in states of high moistness and moderate temperatures. To forestall its event, keeping up with appropriate dispersing between trees to advance air dissemination is fundamental.

Fungicides, both substance and natural, can be applied as a preventive measure during times of high illness pressure. Sulfur-based fungicides are a typical decision for controlling fine buildup, with their viability credited to their capacity to disturb parasitic cell digestion. Then again, neem oil, potassium bicarbonate, and other biofungicides offer natural choices for overseeing fine mold.

Root decay, brought about by different soilborne microbes, for example, Phytophthora spp., represents a danger to the root foundation of jackfruit trees. Unfortunate waste, waterlogged soil, and sullied establishing material can add to the advancement of root decay. Side effects incorporate shrinking, yellowing of leaves, and a decrease in generally tree wellbeing. Carrying out legitimate water the board rehearses, for example, all around depleted establishing destinations and staying away from over-water system, is significant for forestalling root decay.

Soil solarization, a training that includes covering the dirt with straightforward plastic to outfit sun powered heat, is a viable strategy for controlling soilborne microbes. Solarization raises soil temperatures to levels that are deadly to numerous microorganisms, decreasing their populace in the dirt. Furthermore, the utilization of biofungicides containing valuable microorganisms lays out a serious climate for pathogenic organisms.

Leaf spot sicknesses, brought about by different parasitic microorganisms, for example, Cercospora spp. what's more, Alternaria spp., manifest as dim spots on leaves, in the long run prompting defoliation. Leaf spot sicknesses flourish in damp circumstances, and preventive measures incorporate appropriate dividing between trees, ordinary pruning to further develop air dissemination, and the evacuation of contaminated leaves. Fungicides, both substance and natural, can be applied during the developing season to moderate the effect of leaf spot illnesses.

Bug vermin and sicknesses are by all accounts not the only difficulties looked in jackfruit development. Nematodes, tiny worms that live in the dirt, can likewise make harm the underlying foundations of jackfruit trees. Root-hitch nematodes (Meloidogyne spp.) are especially dangerous, prompting the arrangement of nerves on the roots, which obstructs supplement take-up and compromises the tree's general wellbeing. Crop revolution, the utilization of nematode-safe rootstocks, and the use of natural soil corrections are procedures utilized to oversee nematode pervasions.

To address the mind boggling difficulties presented by bugs and illnesses in jackfruit development, a coordinated irritation the executives (IPM) approach is frequently suggested. IPM includes the planned utilization of organic control, social practices, and sensible use of synthetic mediations to limit the effect on the climate and advance manageable farming.

Organic control strategies tackle the force of regular hunters and gainful creatures to oversee bother populaces. Ladybugs, savage scarabs, parasitic wasps, and nematodes are among the partners utilized in organic control techniques. These living beings go after bugs or disturb their life cycles, offering a characteristic and economical method for bug the board.

Social practices envelop a scope of techniques that establish a climate less helpful for nuisance and sickness improvement. These incorporate legitimate disinfection, convenient pruning, crop turn, and the utilization of safe assortments. By cultivating sound plant development and limiting circumstances ideal for irritations and sicknesses, social practices add to the general versatility of the plantation.

Substance intercessions, while a part of nuisance and sickness the executives, are utilized sensibly and if all else fails. Particular and designated utilization of insect poisons, fungicides, and nematicides helps control explicit nuisances and sicknesses without actually hurting excessive non-target creatures. Natural other options, for example, neem-based plans and biopesticides, line up with maintainable agribusiness rehearses.

Preventive estimates assume an essential part in irritation and sickness the board. Normal observing of plantations takes into consideration early recognition of expected issues, empowering convenient intercession. Quarantine measures, for example, assessing and getting establishing material before presentation the plantation, assist with forestalling the spread of bugs and infections. Phytosanitary rehearses add to biosecurity, shielding the plantation from outer dangers.

Inside the unpredictable embroidery of farming, the fight against irritations and infections remains as a never-ending challenge, and jackfruit development is no exemption. This flexible and strong tree, known for its gigantic leafy foods to assorted environments, faces the danger of different bugs and illnesses that can influence its wellbeing and efficiency. Powerful administration techniques, mixing preventive measures, social practices, and prudent utilization of intercessions, are critical for supporting solid jackfruit plantations.

One of the essential foes in the domain of jackfruit development is the jackfruit drill (Bactrocera dorsalis), a natural product fly that lays its eggs on the natural product's surface. The subsequent hatchlings bore into the tissue, causing harm and making passage focuses for optional microbes. Combatting jackfruit drills requires a mix of social and compound control measures.

Socially, ranchers utilize practices, for example, the evacuation and annihilation of plagued natural products to break the vermin's life cycle. Keeping up with plantation sterilization by quickly gathering and discarding fallen organic products diminishes the probability of pervasion. Pheromone traps, decisively positioned, help in observing and controlling grown-up natural product fly populaces by disturbing their mating examples and lessening egg-laying.

Synthetic control includes the occasional use of bug sprays during the fruiting season. The determination of insect sprays considers factors like adequacy, natural effect, and adherence to coordinated bother the executives (IPM) standards. Turning the utilization of various synthetic mixtures is a typical practice to limit the gamble of vermin creating obstruction.

Mealybugs, sap-sucking bugs that swarm leaves, stems, and organic product, are one more typical nuisance in jackfruit development. Their presence can prompt hindered development, shrinking, and a decrease in organic product quality. Coordinated bug the executives techniques for mealybugs incorporate the presentation of regular hunters like ladybugs and parasitic wasps, keeping up with adjusted bug populaces.

Biopesticides, especially those in light of neem oil, act as successful options for mealybug control. Neem disturbs the bug's life cycle, going about as an impediment for taking care of and egg-laying. Moreover, plant oils and insecticidal cleansers offer harmless to the ecosystem choices that limit the effect on useful bugs.

Contagious illnesses represent a huge danger to jackfruit plantations, with anthracnose (Colletotrichum gloeosporioides) standing apart conspicuously. Anthracnose appears as dull sores on leaves, stems, and natural product, prompting untimely organic product drop and decreased attractiveness. Preventive measures incorporate social practices like pruning for air course, expulsion of contaminated plant material, and keeping up with appropriate dividing between trees.

Copper-based fungicides are generally utilized for anthracnose control in regular agribusiness. Notwithstanding, natural other options, for example, biofungicides and neem-based details, offer harmless to the ecosystem choices for infection the board. These natural options line up with supportable horticulture works on, advancing the wellbeing of the plantation environment.

Fine buildup (Oidium spp.) is another contagious illness that can beset jackfruit trees. Described by a white fine substance on leaves, fine buildup represses photosynthesis and compromises generally tree wellbeing. Preventive measures incorporate keeping up with legitimate separating between trees to improve air course, a critical consider forestalling the advancement of fine mold.

Fungicides, both substance and natural, are applied as preventive measures during times of high sickness pressure. Sulfur-based fungicides are generally used to control fine buildup, upsetting contagious cell digestion. Natural other options, including neem oil, potassium bicarbonate, and other biofungicides, give harmless to the ecosystem choices to overseeing fine mold.

Root decay, brought about by soilborne microbes like Phytophthora spp., can represent a danger to the underground root growth of jackfruit trees. Unfortunate waste, waterlogged soil, and tainted establishing material add to the improvement of root decay. Legitimate water the executives rehearses, for example, all around depleted establishing destinations and keeping away from over-water system, are fundamental for forestalling root decay.

Soil solarization, a work on including covering the dirt with straightforward plastic to saddle sunlight based heat, is a viable strategy for controlling soilborne microbes. This cycle raises soil temperatures to levels deadly to numerous microbes, lessening their populace in the dirt. Furthermore, the use of biofungicides containing helpful microorganisms adds to establishing a serious climate for pathogenic organisms.

Leaf spot sicknesses, brought about by different contagious microbes like Cercospora spp. also, Alternaria spp., manifest as dim spots on leaves, in the long run prompting defoliation. These sicknesses flourish in moist circumstances, underlining the significance of preventive estimates like appropriate separating between trees, ordinary pruning for air flow, and the evacuation of contaminated leaves. Fungicides, both synthetic and natural, can be applied during the developing season to relieve the effect of leaf spot infections.

Bug nuisances and sicknesses are not the sole difficulties in jackfruit development. Nematodes, minuscule worms that dwell in the dirt, can make harm the foundations of jackfruit trees. Root-hitch nematodes (Meloidogyne spp.) are especially inconvenient, prompting the development of nerves on the roots, ruining supplement take-up and compromising the tree's general wellbeing.

To oversee nematode invasions, ranchers utilize different procedures. Crop revolution, where jackfruit is exchanged with different yields, assists break the nematode existence with cycling. The utilization of nematode-safe rootstocks and the use of natural soil alterations add to nematode control measures.

Tending to the mind boggling difficulties presented by vermin and illnesses in jackfruit development frequently requires the reception of a coordinated nuisance the board (IPM) approach. This comprehensive technique includes the planned utilization of organic control, social practices, and designated use of substance intercessions to limit natural effect and advance feasible farming.

Organic control strategies influence normal hunters and helpful living beings to oversee bug populaces. Ladybugs, ruthless creepy crawlies, parasitic wasps, and nematodes are among the partners utilized in natural control methodologies. These creatures either go after bugs or upset their life cycles, giving a characteristic and practical method for bother the board.

Social practices assume a critical part in establishing a climate less helpful for vermin and illness improvement. Legitimate disinfection, ideal pruning, crop turn, and the utilization of safe assortments are fundamental parts of social practices. By cultivating sound plant development and limiting circumstances positive for vermin and illnesses, social practices add to the general versatility of the plantation.

Synthetic mediations, while a piece of vermin and infection the executives, are applied sensibly and if all else fails. The particular utilization of insect poisons, fungicides, and nematicides helps control explicit nuisances and infections without really hurting unnecessary non-target organic entities. Natural other options, including neem-based details and biopesticides, line up with economical farming practices.

Preventive estimates assume a urgent part in vermin and sickness the executives. Standard checking of plantations considers early recognition of expected issues, empowering ideal mediation. Quarantine measures, for example, investigating and getting establishing material before presentation the plantation, assist with forestalling the spread of bugs and sicknesses. Phytosanitary rehearses add to biosecurity, safeguarding the plantation from outside dangers.

All in all, the administration of nuisances and illnesses in jackfruit development requires an exhaustive and coordinated approach. Perceiving the different irritations and illnesses that can torment jackfruit trees is the most vital phase in executing powerful control measures. A blend of social practices, natural control strategies, and designated compound mediations, applied reasonably and as one with maintainable farming standards, adds to the strength and efficiency of jackfruit plantations. In the continuous dance among ranchers and the difficulties introduced by vermin and sicknesses, smart and educated techniques guarantee the proceeded with essentialness regarding jackfruit development.

Chapter 4

Blooms of Promise: Jackfruit Blossoms and Pollination

In the tremendous embroidery of nature, where the mind boggling dance of life unfurls, there exists a wonder that frequently gets away from the consideration of easygoing spectators — the sprouting of jackfruit trees. These lofty trees, local to southwestern rainforests of India, give testimony regarding a scene that is both outwardly shocking and environmentally significant — the blooming of jackfruit blossoms and the ensuing system of fertilization.

Jackfruit (Artocarpus heterophyllus) is a tropical tree having a place with the Moraceae family, known for colossal organic products can arrive at shocking sizes. Be that as it may, before these organic products arise, the tree goes through an entrancing regenerative excursion set apart by the development of sensitive blossoms, each holding onto the potential for new life.

The sprouting of jackfruit trees is an ensemble of varieties and fragrances, coordinated ordinarily to draw in the most productive pollinators. The blossoms, with their light yellow petals and unobtrusive scent, make a stunning display inside the thick foliage of the tree. As the blooms spread out, they uncover complex designs that house the conceptive organs significant for the continuation of the species.

The jackfruit blossom is a composite design, made out of both male and female parts. The focal, bulbous district houses the female blossoms, each furnished with a disgrace, style, and ovary. Encompassing these female blossoms are various little, rounded male blossoms, each conveying the fundamental dust delivering organs. This conjunction of male and female components inside a solitary blossom is known as monoecy, a regenerative methodology that has developed to streamline the possibilities of effective fertilization.

The planning of jackfruit blooms is synchronized with the appearance of their essential pollinators — bumble bees. These productive bugs, directed by their natural capacity to recognize flower fragrances and varieties, assume a crucial part in the conceptive outcome of jackfruit trees. As the honey bees accumulate nectar from the blossoms, they unintentionally move dust from the male blossoms to the shame of the female blossoms, working with preparation and the ensuing advancement of jackfruit seeds.

The mutualistic connection between jackfruit trees and bumble bees is a demonstration of the perplexing trap of biological reliance that describes regular environments. The trees give the honey bees a rich wellspring of nectar, while the honey bees, thus, guarantee the trees' regenerative accomplishment by empowering cross-fertilization. This cooperative energy embodies the sensitive equilibrium that supports biodiversity and biological system wellbeing.

The excursion of jackfruit blooms from fertilization to organic product bearing is a demonstration of the flexibility and versatility of nature. When pollinated, the treated ovaries of the female blossoms start to expand and change into youthful jackfruits. These little, green bulges, however unpretentious from the outset, convey the hereditary tradition of the tree and the commitment of people in the future.

As the jackfruits mature, their size and flavor create, changing the once subtle blooms into the notable organic products that have been a staple in the weight control plans of many societies for quite a long time. The flexibility of jackfruit as a culinary fixing, both in its unripe and ready structures, adds one more layer of importance to the tree's regenerative excursion. From exquisite curries to sweet treats, jackfruit rises above culinary limits, mirroring the social variety and innovativeness of the people who integrate it into their dinners.

Past its culinary purposes, jackfruit holds guarantee as an economical and nutritious food source with the possibility to address worldwide food security challenges. With its capacity to flourish in different climatic circumstances and its high healthy benefit, jackfruit presents a chance to expand horticultural practices and improve flexibility despite an evolving environment.

The sprouting of jackfruit trees and the resulting improvement of their natural products likewise offer a window into the more extensive biological elements of tropical rainforests. These trees, with their transcending shelters and rich foliage, add to the perplexing embroidery of life by giving environment and food to a heap of creatures. From bugs that fertilize the blossoms to birds that home in the branches, jackfruit trees act as center points of biodiversity, highlighting the interconnectedness of species inside these environments.

In any case, the excursion of jackfruit blooms and the biological equilibrium they support are not without challenges. Lately, the worldwide decay of pollinators, including honey bees, has raised worries about the manageability of farming and regular environments. Factors, for example, living space misfortune, pesticide use, and environmental change present dangers to pollinator populaces, risking the many-sided dance of fertilization that supports the regenerative progress of plants like jackfruit.

Endeavors to address these difficulties and advance the preservation of pollinators are fundamental for defending the biodiversity and natural strength of our planet. Drives like the assurance of normal territories, reasonable agrarian practices, and the decrease of pesticide use add to establishing conditions where pollinators can flourish. In doing as such, these endeavors benefit the actual pollinators as well as help the multiplication of plants like jackfruit and the innumerable different species that rely upon effective fertilization.

As we wonder about the sprouting of jackfruit trees and the excellence of their blooms, perceiving the more extensive ramifications of this regular spectacle is critical. Past the visual and olfactory charm, the blooms represent the perplexing snare of life, where every species, regardless of how apparently little or subtle, assumes an imperative part in keeping up with the wellbeing and usefulness of environments.

The jackfruit's excursion from bloom to organic product is an account woven into the texture of nature, an account of flexibility, variation, and reliance. It coaxes us to see the value in the marvels of the regular world and highlights the significance of our job as stewards of the climate. In shielding the fragile equilibrium of biological systems, we guarantee that the commitment epitomized in the sprouting jackfruit blooms perseveres for a long time into the future.

All in all, the sprouting of jackfruit trees and the resulting system of fertilization unfurl as a dazzling adventure in the fabulous venue of nature. From the sensitive rise of blooms to the arrangement of fertilization by bumble bees, each stage in the conceptive excursion of jackfruit trees conveys significant biological ramifications.

The monoecious idea of jackfruit blossoms, consolidating both male and female components, mirrors an essential variation to enhance regenerative achievement.

The mutualistic connection between jackfruit trees and bumble bees features the interconnectedness of species and the fundamental job of pollinators in supporting biodiversity. As honey bees move dust from male to female blossoms, the commitment of new life is satisfied, and the excursion from bloom to organic product starts. The change of treated ovaries into youthful jackfruits and their resulting development into the famous, flexible organic products represents the versatility and flexibility of nature.

Past the culinary meaning of jackfruit, its true capacity as an economical and nutritious food source holds guarantee for tending to worldwide food security challenges. The versatility of jackfruit trees to assorted climatic circumstances and their commitment to tropical rainforest environments further highlight their biological significance. Notwithstanding, these environmental elements face dangers from the worldwide decay of pollinators, requiring purposeful endeavors to safeguard and ration these fundamental species.

The blossoming of jackfruit trees welcomes us to consider the more extensive ramifications of our relationship with the normal world. It fills in as a sign of our job as stewards of the climate, liable for defending the fragile equilibrium that supports life on The planet. Drives pointed toward advancing pollinator preservation, maintainable agrarian practices, and territory assurance add to protecting the complex dance of fertilization and guaranteeing the kept sprouting of jackfruit trees and other blooming plants.

Eventually, the tale of jackfruit blooms and fertilization is a story that rises above the limits of individual trees and blossoms. It is a story woven into the texture of environments, where the strings of life entwine in a fragile dance of relationship. The blossoming of jackfruit trees, with its explosions of variety and scent, coaxes us to see the value in the wonders of nature and rouses a pledge to supporting the commitment of life for a long time into the future.

4.1 The flowering process of Jackfruit trees

In the rich scenes of tropical locales, among the heap of greenery that graces the earth, the jackfruit tree (Artocarpus heterophyllus) arises as a natural wonder. Past the great height of its covering and the eminent monstrosity of its natural products, the jackfruit tree is a display during its blossoming interaction — an excursion set apart by unpredictable organic cycles, environmental interdependencies, and commitments of future harvests.

The blooming system of jackfruit trees unfurls with a specific effortlessness, a characteristic movement that starts to enamor spectators as the trees plan to repeat.

Jackfruit trees are local to the rainforests of southwestern India, and their blooming is a demonstration of the transformation and flexibility that have permitted them to flourish in different tropical conditions all over the planet.

The blossoming stage is an essential part in the existence of a jackfruit tree, making way for the ensuing improvement of the notorious jackfruits. This cycle isn't just outwardly shocking yet in addition holds biological importance as it includes the complex dance of fertilization — a pivotal move toward the tree's regenerative excursion.

The blooming of jackfruit trees is a scene described by the development of fragile blossoms that decorate the branches. These blossoms, organized in thick groups, give testimony regarding the transformative procedures that have permitted jackfruit trees to advance their possibilities of fruitful proliferation. Each blossom is a composite design, facilitating both male and female regenerative organs, a peculiarity known as monoecy.

The male and female components inside a solitary blossom act as an essential transformation that upgrades the effectiveness of fertilization. The focal district of the bloom houses the female parts, including the disgrace, style, and ovary, while encompassing it are various little, cylindrical male blossoms containing the fundamental dust creating organs. This conjunction of male and female components inside a similar bloom is a herbal procedure that improves the probability of cross-fertilization, a vital consider the hereditary variety and versatility of the species.

The planning of jackfruit blooms is unpredictably synchronized with the appearance of their essential pollinators — bumble bees. As the blossoms spread out their light yellow petals, they discharge an unobtrusive scent that goes about as a reference point to draw in these enterprising bugs. The bumble bees, drawn by the fragrance and lively shades of the blooms, leave on a rummaging venture that assumes a fundamental part in the conceptive progress of jackfruit trees.

The connection between jackfruit trees and bumble bees is an exemplary illustration of mutualism, a harmonious communication where the two players benefit. The honey bees, as they continued looking for nectar, unintentionally move dust from the male blossoms to the shame of the female blossoms, working with preparation. This unexpected demonstration by the honey bees is a urgent move toward the regenerative cycle, guaranteeing the development of seeds inside the creating jackfruits.

The sprouting of jackfruit trees isn't just a visual scene yet an amicable coordinated effort between the plant world and the bug realm. The sensitive blossoms, influencing in the tropical breeze, become a phase for the artful dance of bumble bees, their persistent fertilization exercises molding the fate of the jackfruit tree and impacting the biodiversity of the encompassing biological system.

As the fertilization cycle unfurls, the prepared ovaries of the female blossoms start to expand, flagging the change of blossoms into youthful jackfruits. These beginning organic products, however at first unnoticeable, convey the hereditary data of the tree and hold the commitment of a future reap. The excursion from fertilization to organic product bearing is a demonstration of the versatility and flexibility of jackfruit trees, which have developed to flourish in different biological specialties.

The development of jackfruits is an enamoring cycle set apart by changes in size, variety, and flavor. From the little, green bulges that arise after fertilization, the jackfruits develop into significant, spiky spheres that hang from the branches. The flexibility of jackfruit as a culinary fixing adds one more layer of importance to its development interaction. In its unripe state, jackfruit fills in as a meat substitute in exquisite dishes, while the ready natural product is delighted in as a sweet treat or integrated into various pastries.

The excursion of jackfruit blooms from fertilization to natural product bearing isn't simply an organic peculiarity yet a social and culinary odyssey that traverses hundreds of years and navigates different foods. In districts where jackfruit is a customary staple, the natural product typifies the rich embroidery of culinary legacy and is profoundly woven into the texture of nearby cooking styles.

Past its social importance, the jackfruit's process holds guarantee as a practical and nutritious food source with the possibility to address worldwide food security challenges. The versatility of jackfruit trees to various environments, combined with the healthy benefit of the natural product, positions it as a suitable choice for expanding farming practices and improving food flexibility despite an evolving environment.

The blossoming of jackfruit trees and the resulting improvement of their natural products add to the more extensive biological elements of tropical rainforests. These transcending trees, with their extensive coverings and lavish foliage, give living space and food to a horde of organic entities. Bugs, birds, and other natural life find shelter in the parts of jackfruit trees, making a microcosm of biodiversity inside the bigger biological system.

Notwithstanding, the excursion of jackfruit blooms and the environmental equilibrium they support face difficulties in the contemporary world. The worldwide decay of pollinators, including honey bees, represents a danger to the mind boggling dance of fertilization that supports the regenerative outcome of plants like jackfruit. Territory misfortune, pesticide use, and environmental change add to the downfall of pollinator populaces, underscoring the dire requirement for preservation endeavors to safeguard these fundamental supporters of biological systems.

Endeavors to address these difficulties stretch out past the insurance of jackfruit trees themselves. Drives focused on pollinator protection, maintainable horticultural practices, and living space rebuilding assume a significant part in supporting the fragile equilibrium of environments. By establishing conditions where pollinators can flourish, we not just defend the regenerative excursion of jackfruit trees yet additionally maintain the biodiversity and flexibility of regular biological systems.

In thinking about the blossoming system of jackfruit trees, we are welcome to ponder the more extensive ramifications of our relationship with nature. The sprouting of jackfruit blooms isn't simply a natural occasion however a story that addresses the interconnectedness of all life on The planet. It highlights the fragile trap of natural connections that support the planet and features our obligation as caretakers of the climate.

The tale of jackfruit blooms and fertilization unfurls as a demonstration of the miracles of the normal world and our job as stewards of the Earth. It prompts us to see the value in the magnificence of biodiversity, perceive the significance of pollinators in supporting environments, and recognize the social and culinary extravagance encapsulated by jackfruit. In doing as such, we are helped to remember the need to proceed with caution in the world, cultivating an amicable concurrence with nature that guarantees the kept blossoming of jackfruit trees and the thriving of life in the entirety of its structures.

4.2 Importance of pollination for fruit development

The perplexing dance of fertilization, a characteristic peculiarity that frequently happens inconspicuous, holds significant significance in the domain of plant generation and organic product improvement. This fundamental natural cycle, organized by different pollinators, is the way in to the continuation of plant species and the creation of organic products that structure a foundation of worldwide biodiversity, farming, and human sustenance.

At its center, fertilization is the exchange of dust — containing male conceptive cells — from the male pieces of a bloom to the female parts, at last prompting treatment. This move can happen inside a similar bloom, a cycle known as self-fertilization, or between blossoms of something similar or various plants, named cross-fertilization. While self-fertilization guarantees propagation, cross-fertilization presents hereditary variety, improving the flexibility and strength of plant populaces.

The meaning of fertilization turns out to be most clear with regards to natural product advancement. Natural products, the full grown ovaries of blossoming plants, act as vessels for seeds and assume a vital part in the dispersal and spread of plant species. The excursion from fertilization to organic product bearing is a mind boggling and captivating story that unfurls across different biological systems and rural scenes.

In the normal world, a huge number of pollinators, going from bugs to birds and even warm blooded creatures, partake in the fertilization cycle. Honey bees, with their specific transformations for gathering dust and nectar, are among the most productive and broad pollinators. Butterflies, moths, bugs, flies, and hummingbirds likewise add to fertilization, each assuming a novel part in unambiguous biological systems.

As these pollinators move from one blossom to another, they coincidentally transport dust, working with the combination of male and female regenerative cells. This demonstration of move isn't simply an organic event; it is a cooperative connection among pollinators and plants. While the pollinators look for sustenance as nectar or dust, they accidentally empower the plants to recreate, guaranteeing the endurance and hereditary variety of plant populaces.

One of the basic results of effective fertilization is the commencement of natural product improvement. When the dust arrives at the disgrace of a blossom and goes down the style to arrive at the ovary, treatment happens. This prepared ovule starts to form into a seed, and the encompassing ovary changes into a natural product. The organic product, fundamentally, is the consequence of a fruitful joint effort between the plant and its pollinators.

Natural products come in different shapes, sizes, and flavors, mirroring the momentous variety of blossoming plants and their variations to explicit biological specialties. From beefy organic products like apples and berries to dry natural products like nuts and grains, the assortment is immense. The structure and design of natural products are complicatedly connected to the techniques for fertilization utilized by the plants that bear them.

In the domain of farming, the significance of fertilization takes on added importance. A considerable lot of the harvests that comprise the underpinning of human eating regimens, including natural products, vegetables, and nuts, depend on fertilization for ideal yield and quality. An impressive number of these harvests are classified as entomophilous, meaning they are subject to bugs for fertilization.

The monetary worth of fertilization in farming is faltering. As indicated by gauges, pollinators add to the development of around 75% of worldwide food crops. Bug pollinated crops alone record for more than $200 billion in yearly worldwide monetary worth. The rundown of monetarily huge yields profiting from fertilization incorporates staples like apples, almonds, blueberries, and watermelon, highlighting the vital job of pollinators in food creation.

Notwithstanding, the worldwide decay of pollinator populaces represents a critical danger to farming efficiency and biodiversity. Factors, for example, living space misfortune, pesticide use, environmental change, and the spread of infections have added to the downfall of pollinators, raising worries about the supportability of food frameworks and the soundness of normal biological systems.

The outcomes of pollinator decline stretch out past the financial domain; they venture into the actual heart of worldwide food security and natural solidness. The perplexing snare of connections among plants and pollinators has developed north of millions of years, bringing about a finely tuned framework that upholds the generation of a huge range of plant species. Disturbances to this framework can have flowing impacts, influencing crop yields as well as the general strength of biological systems.

Endeavors to address the difficulties confronting pollinators include a multilayered approach that envelops protection, feasible farming practices, and mindfulness drives. The security and reclamation of pollinator natural surroundings, decrease in pesticide use, and the advancement of pollinator-accommodating practices in horticulture are urgent strides toward guaranteeing the proceeded with soundness of pollinator populaces.

The significance of fertilization goes past the domains of horticulture and financial matters; it reaches out into the multifaceted embroidery of environments. In normal environments, pollinators add to the multiplication of wild plant species, impacting the elements of plant networks and giving food to a bunch of different creatures. The downfall of pollinators could upset these biological associations, prompting lopsided characteristics in environments and possibly compromising the strength of biodiversity.

The mutualistic connection among plants and pollinators is a demonstration of the interconnectedness of life on The planet. It is a relationship produced through large number of long stretches of coevolution, bringing about a fragile dance of reliance and correspondence. As plants offer nectar and dust as remunerations, pollinators offer the fundamental support of working with generation. This organization is a foundation of natural solidness, adding to the upkeep of sound environments and the arrangement of biological system administrations.

Notwithstanding worldwide difficulties, for example, environmental change, living space misfortune, and biodiversity decline, the significance of fertilization turns out to be much more articulated. Environmental change, specifically, can influence the timing and accessibility of blossoms, upsetting the synchrony among plants and their pollinators. This crisscross could have extreme ramifications for the regenerative progress of plants and, subsequently, for the creatures and people that rely upon them.

The familiarity with the significance of fertilization has filled lately, prompting expanded endeavors to study, preserve, and advance pollinator populaces. Logical examination assumes a pivotal part in understanding the intricacies of fertilization organizations, the variables impacting pollinator wellbeing, and the ramifications of pollinator decline for biological systems and human social orders.

Instructive drives pointed toward bringing issues to light about the job of pollinators, their biological importance, and the activities expected to safeguard them add to encouraging a feeling of obligation and stewardship. Pollinator-accommodating cultivating rehearses, resident science ventures, and local area commitment endeavors further engage people to assume a part in supporting pollinator wellbeing and protection.

All in all, the significance of fertilization for natural product advancement stretches out a long ways past the singular blossoms and plants engaged with this complex dance. It envelops the worldwide snare of biodiversity, horticulture, and biological systems that depend on the administrations given by pollinators. From the generation of wildflowers in regular natural surroundings to the creation of staple harvests in farming, the job of fertilization is crucial.

As we explore the difficulties of a quickly influencing world, the need to defend pollinators and their living spaces turns into a common obligation. Preservation endeavors, supportable rural practices, and public mindfulness are fundamental parts of an all encompassing way to deal with safeguarding the fragile equilibrium that supports life on The planet. In perceiving the significance of fertilization, we recognize the interconnectedness of every single residing thing and embrace our job as stewards of a planet where the prospering of plants, creatures, and people is unpredictably connected to the strength of pollinator populaces and the biological systems they support.

4.3 Natural and artificial pollination methods

In the complex universe of plant proliferation, the strategies for fertilization assume a crucial part in molding the variety and wealth of vegetation across environments. Normal fertilization, coordinated by different vectors like breeze, water, and creatures, has been the foundation of plant regenerative methodologies for a long period of time. In any case, as human exercises and farming practices have advanced, fake fertilization strategies have arisen to address explicit requirements in crop creation and biodiversity preservation. The unique exchange among normal and counterfeit fertilization techniques highlights the intricacy of overseeing plant generation in a quickly impacting world.

Normal fertilization, driven by transformative cycles, includes the exchange of dust from the male regenerative organs of a blossom to the female conceptive organs, eventually prompting treatment and the improvement of seeds. This cycle is intervened by a different cluster of pollinators, each adjusted to explicit environmental specialties and plant species. The coevolution among plants and their pollinators has brought about a surprising variety of botanical transformations and pollinator systems, making unpredictable organizations of mutualistic connections.

Wind fertilization, or anemophily, is a typical normal fertilization strategy saw in many plant species. Plants adjusted to wind fertilization frequently produce enormous amounts of lightweight, airborne dust. Grasses, conifers, and certain blooming plants, like prairie species, depend on the breeze to scatter their dust over impressive distances. While wind fertilization is energy-proficient for plants, it is a moderately unpredictable strategy, depending on possibility experiences among dust and the open marks of disgrace of blossoms.

Water fertilization, or hydrophily, is another normal fertilization strategy, though more uncommon than anemophily. Sea-going plants, especially those lowered or drifting on the water's surface, discharge their dust into the water. The flows then transport the dust to responsive female blossoms. Water fertilization is most common in oceanic environments, where the development of water fills in as the essential vector for dust dispersal. Water lilies and a few seagrasses embody plant species that utilize water fertilization.

Creature fertilization, or zoophily, is maybe the most complex and broadened type of regular fertilization. This technique depends on creatures — fundamentally bugs, birds, and warm blooded animals — to move dust between blossoms. The visual and olfactory signs of blossoms draw in these creatures, which, thus, acquire nectar, dust, or different compensations from the blossoms. The coevolution among plants and their creature pollinators has brought about a surprising cluster of transformations, including blossom morphology, tinge, and fragrance, customized to draw in unambiguous pollinator gatherings.

Honey bees, with their specific variations for gathering dust and nectar, are among the most proficient and boundless bug pollinators. Their bristly bodies and concentrated structures, like dust bushels on their rear legs, work with the exchange of dust as they move from one bloom to another. Butterflies, with their long proboscis, are drawn to blossoms with rounded structures, while moths, dynamic during the evening, fertilize blossoms that sprout at night. Hummingbirds, bats, and, surprisingly, little warm blooded animals add to fertilization, each with remarkable variations fit to their particular natural jobs.

While normal fertilization components have been viable for centuries, anthropogenic exercises and changes in land use have acquainted difficulties with these cycles. Living space misfortune, pesticide use, environmental change, and the decay of pollinator populaces are among the elements undermining the fragile equilibrium of normal fertilization organizations. Because of these difficulties, counterfeit fertilization strategies have been created to address explicit necessities in farming, cultivation, and protection.

Counterfeit fertilization includes human mediation to physically move dust between blossoms. This strategy is utilized in circumstances where regular fertilization is lacking or unrealistic. In horticulture, where harvest yield and quality are of principal significance, counterfeit fertilization

is frequently used to guarantee a dependable and predictable gather. Certain yields, for example, natural product trees, vegetables, and nuts, may profit from advantageous or completely counterfeit fertilization techniques.

One normal fake fertilization technique includes the utilization of brushes or implements to move dust between blossoms. In organic product plantations, for instance, where enormous monoculture plantings might restrict normal fertilization, laborers use brushes to gather dust from the male blossoms of one tree and apply it to the female blossoms of another. This interaction imitates the activity of regular pollinators, guaranteeing that the dust arrives at the responsive disgrace and treatment can happen.

At times, especially in nursery development or controlled horticultural conditions, producers might depend on the utilization of blowers or fans to scatter dust. This strategy is successful for crops that are managable to twist fertilization in their normal territories. The controlled dispersal of dust as such takes into consideration exact fertilization timing and expanded command over the regenerative cycle.

For specific yields, especially those with complex blossom structures or concentrated fertilization necessities, hand fertilization is a fastidious yet compelling strategy. Talented specialists physically move dust from male to female blossoms utilizing devices like fine brushes or tweezers. This technique is usually utilized in the development of high-esteem crops like vanilla orchids, where the complexities of bloom life systems require cautious human mediation.

While counterfeit fertilization strategies have demonstrated important in improving harvest yields and guaranteeing food security, they are not without challenges. The work escalated nature of some counterfeit fertilization practices can be financially restrictive, especially for limited scope ranchers. Also, the dependence on counterfeit techniques may not address the underlying drivers of pollinator decline, for example, living space misfortune and pesticide use, which have more extensive biological ramifications.

In the domain of preservation, counterfeit fertilization strategies are once in a while utilized to help the generation of jeopardized plant species. In greenhouses, analysts might utilize methods like hand fertilization to create seeds for the proliferation of uncommon or compromised plants. These endeavors add to ex-situ preservation, saving hereditary variety beyond the plants' local environments.

Notwithstanding, counterfeit fertilization in preservation endeavors faces moral and commonsense contemplations. Mediations to help the proliferation of jeopardized species may coincidentally disturb normal biological cycles, and the progress of fake fertilization in cultivating the drawn out endurance of an animal groups stays dependent upon resolving more extensive issues, like natural surroundings rebuilding and security.

The reconciliation of regular and counterfeit fertilization techniques features the dynamic and advancing nature of plant generation the executives. While regular fertilization components have molded the variety of vegetation for a long period of time, the difficulties presented by human exercises require versatile procedures. The cautious thought of environmental standards, combined with mechanical developments, takes into consideration a nuanced approach that looks to adjust the advantages of both regular and fake fertilization.

Even with worldwide difficulties, for example, environmental change, living space misfortune, and the downfall of pollinators, there is a dire requirement for comprehensive ways to deal with help fertilization organizations. Preservation endeavors zeroed in on safeguarding regular living spaces, diminishing pesticide use, and advancing pollinator-accommodating practices in agribusiness are pivotal for guaranteeing the flexibility of environments. All the while, progressions in fake fertilization strategies can add to improving rural efficiency and tending to food security concerns.

The moral components of controlling fertilization processes, whether for rural or preservation purposes, highlight the significance of thinking about the more extensive environmental setting. The sensitive equilibrium of biological systems depends on the exchange of endless species, each with a job in forming the biodiversity and usefulness of the normal world. As we explore the intricacies of overseeing plant propagation, it is fundamental for approach these intercessions with lowliness, regard for natural cycles, and a promise to safeguarding the multifaceted connections that support life on The planet.

4.4 Maximizing fruit yield through effective pollination

Boosting natural product yield through successful fertilization remains as a basic part of practical horticulture, guaranteeing the wealth of different harvests that add to worldwide food security. Fertilization, the exchange of dust from male to female regenerative organs in blooming plants, is a characteristic cycle fundamental for the development of seeds and natural products. A heap of variables, including the presence and action of pollinators, natural circumstances, and plant qualities, impacts the viability of fertilization in farming settings.

The dependence of many harvests on fertilization for natural product advancement highlights the reliance among plants and pollinators. Honey bees, butterflies, birds, and different pollinators assume necessary parts in cultivating the multiplication of various plant species. Understanding the complexities of fertilization instruments and carrying out techniques to upgrade fertilization productivity are fundamental for advancing natural product yield and guaranteeing the manageability of rural frameworks.

One basic thought in augmenting organic product yield is the ID and conservation of regular pollinator living spaces. Wild pollinators, like honey bees and butterflies, frequently assume significant parts in horticultural scenes by adding to the fertilization of yields. In any case, factors, for example, environment misfortune, pesticide use, and environmental change present dangers to pollinator populaces. Preserving normal living spaces, including wildflower-rich regions and different environments, gives fundamental settling locales and search for pollinators, cultivating their wellbeing and overflow.

As well as supporting regular pollinators, producers can carry out systems to draw in and support different pollinator networks inside horticultural scenes. Establishing cover crops, laying out hedgerows, and integrating blossoming plants inside and around fields set out scrounging open doors and settling locales for pollinators. This methodology, known as agroecological configuration, upgrades biodiversity inside agrarian settings, adding to the flexibility of pollinator populaces and further developing natural product yield.

The planning of blossoming inside crops is a basic component impacting the progress of fertilization. Coordination between plant blossoming periods and the movement of pollinators is fundamental for augmenting organic product set. Producers can choose crop assortments and cultivars with covering blossoming periods, guaranteeing that male and female blossoms are responsive simultaneously. Also, observing neighborhood environment conditions and occasional varieties takes into account ideal timing of planting to synchronize blossoming with top pollinator action.

The utilization of overseen pollinators, like bumble bees, honey bees, and other honey bee species, is a typical practice in horticulture to upgrade fertilization proficiency. Beekeeping and the situation of colonies of bees in or close to edit fields give a dependable and concentrated labor force of pollinators. Nonetheless, the viability of overseen pollinators depends on appropriate administration works on, including hive wellbeing, sufficient sustenance, and contemplations for likely adverse consequences on wild pollinator populaces.

Guaranteeing a different and sound eating regimen for oversaw pollinators is significant for their essentialness and effectiveness in fertilization. Establishing different blooming crops and giving supplemental scrounge, for example, wildflowers or cover crops, improves the wholesome assets accessible to pollinators. In addition, decreasing the utilization of synthetic pesticides and deciding on coordinated bug the executives rehearses safeguards the wellbeing of both oversaw and wild pollinators, cultivating more compelling fertilization.

Certain farming practices include the expulsion of inefficient blossoms to focus assets on creating organic products. This interaction, known as natural product diminishing, is frequently utilized to improve the size and nature of collected natural products.

While organic product diminishing can add to higher natural product yield, cautious thought is expected to try not to eliminate over the top quantities of blossoms, which could adversely influence fertilization and ensuing organic product advancement. Finding some kind of harmony between organic product diminishing and fertilization prerequisites is fundamental for accomplishing ideal yields.

The reception of accuracy farming advancements offers new chances to streamline fertilization and natural product yield. Remote detecting advancements, for example, drones outfitted with sensors or satellites, can give significant bits of knowledge into crop wellbeing, blossoming examples, and fertilization elements. This data empowers producers to pursue information driven choices, changing administration rehearses progressively to boost natural product yield while limiting ecological effects.

Environmental change presents difficulties to farming frameworks, influencing temperature examples, precipitation, and the dispersion of pollinators. Understanding the expected effects of environmental change on fertilization elements is fundamental for creating versatile procedures. For example, changing establishing plans, choosing environment strong harvest assortments, and carrying out water the executives practices can assist with moderating the impacts of environmental change on fertilization and organic product yield.

Hereditary upgrades in crop assortments offer one more road for expanding natural product yield through improved fertilization. Reproducing programs zeroed in on creating cultivars with characteristics like expanded blossom engaging quality, delayed blooming periods, and further developed dust suitability add to more effective fertilization and higher organic product set. Tackling hereditary variety inside yields can prompt the improvement of assortments more qualified to winning ecological circumstances and pollinator accessibility.

Examination into the improvement of fertilization strategies keeps on progressing, with continuous investigations investigating imaginative ways to deal with upgrade organic product yield. For instance, the utilization of entomophilous robots furnished with dust distributors has been examined as a likely device for fake fertilization. While these advancements are still in their beginning phases, they feature the continuous endeavors to coordinate state of the art arrangements into horticulture, guaranteeing the proceeded with outcome of fertilization and organic product improvement.

Past the extent of ordinary agribusiness, reasonable and regenerative cultivating rehearses focus on the improvement of pollinator territories and the advancement of biodiversity. Agroforestry, permaculture, and biological cultivating frameworks coordinate pollinator-accommodating works on, recognizing the interconnectedness between horticultural scenes and normal environments. These methodologies focus on natural flexibility, advancing fertilization administrations as a central part of manageable food creation.

All in all, expanding organic product yield through powerful fertilization requires a comprehensive and versatile methodology that thinks about the complex connections between plants, pollinators, and the more extensive climate. Rationing normal pollinator territories, supporting assorted pollinator networks, and carrying out agroecological plan standards add to the strength of fertilization organizations. Coordination of blossoming periods, the utilization of overseen pollinators, and the reception of accuracy agribusiness innovations further upgrade the productivity of fertilization and natural product set.

Adjusting organic product diminishing practices, environmental change variations, and hereditary upgrades in crop assortments guarantees that farming remaining parts receptive to advancing difficulties. Continuous investigation into creative fertilization techniques, for example, drone-helped fertilization, exhibits the potential for innovative progressions to supplement conventional methodologies. At last, the quest for maintainable and regenerative cultivating rehearses places fertilization at the front, perceiving its vital job in accomplishing ideal organic product yield while defending the soundness of biological systems. As horticulture explores the intricacies of the advanced world, the obligation to compelling fertilization rehearses becomes principal, guaranteeing the overflow of organic products that sustain the two individuals and the planet.

Chapter 5

Fruitful Harvest: Jackfruit Development Stages

The excursion of jackfruit, from its unassuming starting points as a seed to its summit as an experienced organic product, is an entrancing investigation of nature's unpredictable cycles. In the core of tropical locales, where the sun's glow and plentiful precipitation establish the ideal climate, jackfruit trees flourish. These monsters of the natural product world, having a place with the Moraceae family, gradually rise up out of the dirt, their process set apart by unmistakable formative stages.

The excursion starts with the germination of the jackfruit seed. The seed, encased inside a defensive coat, enthusiastically ingests dampness from the earth. As water infiltrates the seed coat, the undeveloped organism inside grows and becomes fully awake. This denotes the origin of another jackfruit tree. The undeveloped shoot lengthens, going after the daylight that channels through the rich overhang above. Minuscule roots stretch out descending, securing the youthful plant to the ground.

In the beginning phases of development, the jackfruit sapling is especially helpless. It depends on the supplements put away inside the seed for food. As the roots dive further into the dirt, they lay out an organization that works with the take-up of water and fundamental minerals. The youthful tree's leaves spread out, showing their dynamic green shades. These leaves act as the essential site for photosynthesis, the cycle by which the plant saddles daylight to create energy.

As time passes, the jackfruit tree develops, progressively changing from a fragile sapling to a solid adolescent. The storage compartment thickens, offering underlying help to the extending shade of leaves. This stage is critical for the plant's turn of events, as it establishes the groundwork for the productive blossoming and fruiting stages that lie ahead. The tree, presently outfitted with a strong root foundation and durable trunk, is ready to channel its energy into generation.

The jackfruit tree enters its blossoming stage, an exhibition of nature's masterfulness. Bunches of minuscule, fragrant roses rise up out of the tree's limbs, drawing in pollinators like honey bees and butterflies. The blossoms, either male or female, convey the potential for new life. The male blossoms discharge dust out of sight, wanting to track down their direction to the responsive disgrace of the female blossoms. This complex dance of nature guarantees the effective fertilization of the jackfruit blooms.

Upon fruitful fertilization, the female blossoms change into little, spiky designs known as jackfruit buds. These buds grow in size, and their spines bit by bit relax, uncovering the arising jackfruit inside. The creating organic product is safeguarded by a thick, green external skin, which fills in as a safeguard against ecological elements and likely hunters. As the jackfruit keeps on developing, the tree designates assets to support the extending organic product, coordinating supplements from the dirt through its vascular framework.

The developing jackfruit goes through a wonderful change, developing both in size and appearance. The green skin turns out to be more articulated, and the spiky outside gives way to a smoother surface. The size of the natural product can change altogether, impacted by elements like the tree's age, ecological circumstances, and the accessibility of supplements. A few jackfruits accomplish significant aspects, procuring them the title of the world's biggest organic product.

As the jackfruit moves toward its pinnacle readiness, unobtrusive changes happen in its tone and fragrance. The once lively green outside embraces a yellowish shade, flagging the natural product's preparation for gather. The smell strengthens, delivering a sweet and tropical scent that coaxes those close by. The excursion that started with a minuscule seed has now finished in the realization of a completely evolved and mature jackfruit.

The gathering of jackfruit is a pivotal event, denoting the perfection of long stretches of development and improvement. The planning of the gather is basic, as it decides the organic product's flavor, surface, and generally quality. Gathering too soon may bring about an immature natural product, coming up short on the trademark pleasantness and smell. Then again, postponing the reap may prompt overripeness, influencing both taste and surface.

The gathering system includes cautiously withdrawing the jackfruit from its stem, guaranteeing negligible harm to the products of the soil tree. The sheer size and weight of certain jackfruits require the utilization of particular devices and procedures. When gathered, the jackfruit is prepared to leave on the following period of its excursion — the excursion from tree to table.

Jackfruit's flexibility in the culinary world is unrivaled. Its tissue, with a stringy and substantial surface, fits a heap of culinary applications. From appetizing dishes to sweet treats, jackfruit has tracked down its direction into different foods all over the planet. The ready, sweet tissue is a well known fixing in treats, smoothies, and jams, while the unripe, youthful jackfruit is valued for its capacity to imitate the surface of meat in exquisite dishes.

In many societies, jackfruit holds social and representative importance. It fills in as a staple food source, giving food to networks in tropical districts. The jackfruit tree itself offers significant assets, with its wood being utilized for development and its leaves for different customary practices. Past its substantial commitments, jackfruit conveys a rich social story, woven into the texture of culinary customs and fables.

The excursion of jackfruit reaches out past the singular tree and natural product, enveloping environmental and farming aspects. Jackfruit trees assume a significant part in agroforestry frameworks, adding to biodiversity and soil wellbeing. The trees' broad underground roots assist with forestalling soil disintegration, and their enormous, spreading shelters give shade to different yields. Also, jackfruit trees show versatility even with changing ecological circumstances, making them significant resources in supportable cultivating rehearses.

As the worldwide interest for manageable and plant-based food choices keeps on rising, jackfruit has earned consideration as a suitable and eco-accommodating other option. Its capacity to flourish in different environments, combined with its wholesome profile, positions jackfruit as a versatile and feasible harvest. The development of jackfruit offers monetary open doors for ranchers as well as adds to the more extensive objective of making a more economical and strong food framework.

The excursion of jackfruit — from seed to gather — is a demonstration of the multifaceted dance of nature, where each stage assumes a urgent part in the organic product's turn of events. From the germination of a minuscule seed to the rise of a strong tree, and from the sensitive blooms to the vigorous organic product, each stage adds to the making of a plentiful gather.

The flexibility of jackfruit, both in the kitchen and in agroforestry frameworks, highlights its importance as a significant and feasible asset.

Taking everything into account, the tale of jackfruit is one of development, versatility, and overflow. It is a story written in the dirt, sung by the stirring leaves, and celebrated in the kitchens of different societies. The excursion from seed to reap is an embroidery woven with the strings of nature's insight and human resourcefulness. As we enjoy the kinds of ready jackfruit or relish the exquisite notes of a jackfruit curry, let us value the excursion that carried this surprising natural product to our tables — an excursion that keeps on unfurling in plantations and homesteads all over the planet, promising a productive collect for a long time into the future.

5.1 Tracking the stages of Jackfruit development

The excursion of jackfruit, an exceptional tropical natural product, unfurls in unmistakable stages, each adding to the organic product's turn of events and possible collect. The story of jackfruit starts with a little seed, holding onto the potential for development and change. Settled inside its defensive coat, the jackfruit seed enthusiastically retains dampness from the dirt, starting the course of germination. As water infiltrates the seed coat, the incipient organism inside grows, flagging the enlivening of life.

Starting here of germination, a fragile jackfruit sapling arises, arriving at upward in quest for daylight. Small roots stretch out into the dirt, securing the youthful plant and laying out an establishment for its future development. In these beginning phases, the sapling depends on the supplements put away inside the seed for food, a significant period that establishes the vibe for its turn of events.

As the sapling develops into an adolescent tree, the storage compartment thickens, offering underlying help for the blossoming covering of leaves. The leaves, with their energetic green shades, become the essential locales for photosynthesis — a key cycle by which the plant changes over daylight into energy. This period of development is critical, as it readies the jackfruit tree for the regenerative stages that will follow.

The blossoming stage denotes an exhibition in the existence of the jackfruit tree. Groups of small, fragrant blossoms enhance its branches, drawing in pollinators like honey bees and butterflies. These blossoms, either male or female, hold the way in to the tree's conceptive achievement. The male blossoms discharge dust out of sight, wanting to track down their direction to the open shame of the female blossoms. This unpredictable dance of nature guarantees the effective fertilization of the jackfruit blooms, making way for the following stage.

Following fruitful fertilization, the female blossoms change into little, spiky designs known as jackfruit buds. These buds enlarge in size, and their spines bit by bit mellow, uncovering the arising jackfruit inside. The creating natural product is safeguarded by a thick, green external skin, which fills in as a safeguard against ecological elements and likely hunters. The tree assigns assets to feed the developing natural product, coordinating fundamental supplements from the dirt through its vascular framework.

The developing jackfruit goes through a striking change in both size and appearance. The green skin turns out to be more articulated, and the spiky outside gives way to a smoother surface. The size of the natural product can differ essentially, impacted by elements like the tree's age, ecological circumstances, and supplement accessibility. A few jackfruits achieve significant aspects, procuring them the qualification of being the world's biggest organic product.

As the jackfruit moves toward its pinnacle readiness, unpretentious changes happen in its tone and smell. The once dynamic green outside takes on a yellowish shade, flagging the natural product's status for gather. The smell strengthens, delivering a sweet and tropical scent that coaxes those close by. The excursion that started with a minuscule seed has now finished in the realization of a completely evolved and mature jackfruit, fit to be reaped.

The reaping of jackfruit is an earth shattering event, denoting the finish of long stretches of development and improvement. The planning of the reap is basic, as it decides the natural product's flavor, surface, and by and large quality. Gathering too soon may bring about an immature natural product, without the trademark pleasantness and smell. On the other hand, deferring the collect might prompt overripeness, influencing both taste and surface.

The gathering system includes cautious separation of the jackfruit from its stem, limiting harm to both the leafy foods tree. The sheer size and weight of certain jackfruits require the utilization of particular devices and methods. When gathered, the jackfruit is prepared to leave on the following period of its excursion — the excursion from tree to table.

Jackfruit's adaptability in the culinary world is unparalleled. Its tissue, with a sinewy and substantial surface, fits a bunch of culinary applications. From exquisite dishes to sweet treats, jackfruit has tracked down its direction into assorted foods all over the planet. The ready, sweet tissue is a well known fixing in treats, smoothies, and jams, while the unripe, youthful jackfruit is valued for its capacity to emulate the surface of meat in flavorful dishes.

In many societies, jackfruit holds social and emblematic importance. It fills in as a staple food source, giving food to networks in tropical locales. The jackfruit tree itself offers important assets, with its wood being utilized for development and its leaves for different conventional practices. Past its substantial commitments, jackfruit conveys a rich social story, woven into the texture of culinary customs and legends.

The excursion of jackfruit stretches out past the singular tree and natural product, incorporating environmental and agrarian aspects. Jackfruit trees assume an essential part in agroforestry frameworks, adding to biodiversity and soil wellbeing. The trees' broad underground roots assist with forestalling soil disintegration, and their enormous, spreading overhangs give shade to different yields. Also, jackfruit trees exhibit strength even with changing natural circumstances, making them significant resources in feasible cultivating rehearses.

As the worldwide interest for supportable and plant-based food choices keeps on rising, jackfruit has gathered consideration as a suitable and eco-accommodating other option. Its capacity to flourish in different environments, combined with its nourishing profile, positions jackfruit as a versatile and manageable yield. The development of jackfruit offers monetary open doors for ranchers as well as adds to the more extensive objective of making a more supportable and strong food framework.

The excursion of jackfruit — from seed to collect — is a demonstration of the perplexing dance of nature, where each stage assumes a pivotal part in the organic product's turn of events. From the germination of a minuscule seed to the development of a strong tree, and from the fragile blooms to the powerful natural product, each stage adds to the formation of a plentiful collect. The flexibility of jackfruit, both in the kitchen and in agroforestry frameworks, highlights its importance as a significant and maintainable asset.

Taking everything into account, the narrative of jackfruit is one of development, strength, and overflow. It is a story written in the dirt, sung by the stirring leaves, and celebrated in the kitchens of different societies. The excursion from seed to reap is an embroidery woven with the strings of nature's insight and human resourcefulness. As we enjoy the kinds of ready jackfruit or relish the flavorful notes of a jackfruit curry, let us value the excursion that carried this surprising natural product to our tables — an excursion that keeps on unfurling in plantations and ranches all over the planet, promising a productive gather for a long time into the future.

5.2 Recognizing when the fruit is ready for harvest

Perceiving when an organic product is prepared for collect is a craftsmanship and a science that ranchers and cultivators have sharpened over ages. This significant expertise is especially obvious on account of jackfruit, a tropical monster that goes through a progression of changes flagging its readiness. Jackfruit, known for its huge size and flexible culinary purposes, gives visual and olfactory signs to direct the gathering system.

One of the essential signs of a jackfruit's preparation for reap is its size. While jackfruits can differ broadly in aspects in light of variables, for example, the tree's age and developing circumstances, there is a general expansion in size as the natural product develops.

Youthful jackfruits are recognizably more modest, and as they progress through the formative stages, they go through a huge development in both length and circumference. This development is demonstrative of the organic product gathering the sugars and supplements important for a tasty and fulfilling eating experience.

Variety is one more key viewable signal while deciding the readiness of a jackfruit. The organic product's outside goes through a groundbreaking excursion from green to yellow as it develops. In its beginning phases, the jackfruit sports a dynamic green tone, mixing in with the foliage of the tree. As it approaches readiness, an unobtrusive yellowing starts to assume control over, flagging the gathering of normal sugars. This adjustment of variety is an obvious sign that the jackfruit is entering a stage where its flavors are probably going to be more evolved and pleasant.

The surface of the jackfruit's outside likewise develops during the maturing system. Youthful jackfruits have a spiky, firm external surface that fills in as a defensive layer. As the organic product develops, the spines relax, and the general surface becomes smoother. Running one's hands over the surface can give significant data about the organic product's progressive phase. A developed jackfruit will have a less inflexible feel, showing that the interior tissue has gone through the fundamental changes for ideal taste and surface.

Fragrance assumes a urgent part in checking the readiness of many organic products, and jackfruit is no exemption. As the organic product advances toward development, it transmits a sweet and tropical scent that is unquestionable. The fragrance heightens as the jackfruit arrives at its pinnacle readiness, making an olfactory encounter that is in many cases the principal sign for collectors. The captivating fragrance isn't just a sign for people yet in addition effectively draws in creatures that could help with seed dispersal, featuring the complex connection between the products of the soil climate.

Contact turns into an important device in the evaluation of jackfruit readiness. A delicate push on the natural product can uncover its solidness and versatility. A full grown jackfruit ought to yield somewhat to pressure, showing that the tissue inside has mellowed and fostered the ideal surface. Be that as it may, it's crucial for work out some kind of harmony — extreme non-abrasiveness could show overripeness, influencing the nature of the organic product.

Noticing the stem or peduncle of the jackfruit gives extra bits of knowledge into its readiness. As the organic product develops, the stem interfacing it to the tree goes through changes. In certain assortments, the stem might begin to evaporate or change tone, proposing that the jackfruit is done getting supplements from the tree. This regular separation process is a natural sign that the organic product is fit to be gathered.

While these visual, olfactory, and material signals are significant markers, the particular qualities of a ready jackfruit can fluctuate among various assortments. Nearby information, went down through ages, frequently assumes an essential part in tweaking the collecting system. Experienced ranchers foster a natural comprehension of the remarkable elements of the jackfruit assortments they develop, permitting them to arrive at nuanced conclusions about the ideal time for collect.

Timing is a basic consider guaranteeing the nature of the jackfruit. Reaping too soon may bring about an immature organic product with deficient sugars and flavors. Then again, deferring the reap can prompt overripeness, causing changes in surface and taste that may not be attractive. The test lies in figuring out the perfect balance, the second when the jackfruit has arrived at its pinnacle readiness, offering an amicable mix of flavors, smells, and surfaces.

The gathering system itself requires accuracy and care. Jackfruits are frequently appended to solid branches, and their weight can make separation testing. Customary techniques include the utilization of long shafts with sharp edges or sickles toward the end, permitting gatherers to cut the stem while limiting harm to the natural product. Specific apparatuses and gear have likewise been created to work with the effective and safe reaping of jackfruit, perceiving its novel attributes and size.

When collected, the jackfruit's process go on as it is shipped to business sectors, kitchens, and tables. The ready natural product, with its tempting fragrance and dynamic tone, turns into a culinary material for a different scope of dishes. From sweet pastries to flavorful curries, jackfruit's adaptability sparkles in different cooking styles all over the planet.

All in all, perceiving when a jackfruit is prepared for gather is a nuanced and multi-tactile cycle. Cultivators influence a mix of visual, olfactory, and material prompts, alongside their insight into explicit assortments, to settle on informed conclusions about the ideal chance to pick the natural product. This expertise, frequently went down through ages, is a demonstration of the personal association among ranchers and the land they develop. As jackfruit keeps on catching the consideration of culinary fans and manageability advocates, the craft of reaping this tropical monster stays an imperative part of its excursion from tree to table.

5.3 Harvesting techniques and tools

The collecting of organic products is a sensitive and urgent stage in the rural cycle, and jackfruit, with its enormous size and weight, requests exceptional consideration and explicit methods. Ranchers utilize different devices and techniques to guarantee the productive and safe reaping of jackfruit, a cycle that includes accuracy, experience, and a profound comprehension of the organic product's qualities.

One of the essential difficulties in gathering jackfruit lies in its significant weight. Mature jackfruits can weigh anyplace from a couple of kilograms to more than 30 kilograms, contingent upon variables like the tree's age, assortment, and developing circumstances. Given the size and mass of the organic product, cautious thought is expected to abstain from harm during the reaping system. Customary techniques frequently include the utilization of long shafts with a cutting carry out toward the end.

Shaft reaping is a generally utilized procedure, particularly in locales where jackfruit development is predominant. The long posts, frequently made of bamboo or lightweight metal, are furnished with a sharp edge or sickle toward one side. Collectors cautiously position the state of the art around the stem of the jackfruit and make an exact slice to isolate it from the tree. This technique takes into consideration a level of distance between the reaper and the natural product, decreasing the gamble of injury or harm.

At times, where the level of the tree represents a test, stepping stools are utilized to arrive at the higher branches conveying the developed jackfruits. The utilization of stepping stools requires extra expertise and mindfulness, as the reaper should keep up with equilibrium and strength while controlling the post for gathering. Wellbeing measures, for example, getting the stepping stool and wearing fitting defensive stuff, are fundamental to limit gambles during the gathering system.

As innovation propels, there has been a developing interest in creating particular devices for jackfruit collecting. Reaping apparatuses planned explicitly for jackfruit expect to improve productivity, lessen actual burden on gatherers, and limit the potential for harm to the organic product. These instruments frequently include adaptive posts, taking into account flexible reach to oblige differing tree levels and natural product positions.

One such advancement is the electric or battery-fueled post saw, which consolidates the advantages of customary shaft reaping with the accommodation of motorization. These devices normally include a trimming tool or pruning sharp edge toward the finish of an extendable shaft. The gatherer have some control over the cutting activity from a distance, making it simpler to arrive at higher branches without the requirement for stepping stools. Electric shaft saws offer a harmony among productivity and decreased actual effort.

Mechanical reapers address one more road of advancement in jackfruit collecting. These machines are intended to smooth out the cycle, especially in business plantations where the size of development might be broad. Mechanical collectors frequently integrate transport frameworks or assortment canisters to effectively assemble the reaped natural products. While these machines can possibly essentially increment efficiency, their reception might be restricted by variables like expense, support prerequisites, and the requirement for particular preparation.

In districts where jackfruit is a customary and resource crop, the utilization of straightforward and manual devices endures. Cleavers or enormous blades are normal executes for slicing through the stem of the jackfruit. While manual apparatuses require actual exertion and expertise, they stay available and viable for limited scope ranchers with restricted assets.

The planning of the reap is a basic part of the cycle, impacting the quality and taste of the jackfruit. Gathering too soon may result in an underripe natural product, without the ideal pleasantness and flavor. Then again, postponing the gather can prompt overripeness, influencing the surface and taste. Experienced ranchers depend on a mix of visual, olfactory, and material signals to decide the ideal time for reaping.

The stem or peduncle, which interfaces the jackfruit to the tree, likewise gives important data about its status for gather. As the natural product develops, changes happen in the stem, for example, drying or a change in variety. Noticing these progressions assists ranchers with distinguishing when the jackfruit has normally segregated from the tree or is prepared to be physically collected.

When the jackfruit is disconnected, care should be taken during dealing with and transportation to forestall harm. The natural product's external surface, however powerful, can be helpless to swelling or penetrates. Guaranteeing that the jackfruits are tenderly positioned in holders or crates, ideally with padding materials, helps protect their quality during transport.

Post-gather dealing with rehearses assume a vital part in keeping up with the newness and attractiveness of jackfruit. Legitimate capacity conditions, including temperature and mugginess control, are fundamental to expand the timeframe of realistic usability of the reaped organic products. At times, ranchers might apply coatings or wraps to the jackfruits to make a defensive layer that decreases dampness misfortune and limits actual harm.

In business settings, the collected jackfruits go through an arranging cycle to classify them in light of size, quality, and readiness. This arranging guarantees that the natural products fulfill the guidelines for different market channels, whether they are bound for neighborhood markets, supermarkets, or handling offices. Consistency in size and quality upgrades the market allure of jackfruit and works with appropriation.

The market interest for jackfruit has extended past new utilization, prompting expanded revenue in handling and worth added items. Handled jackfruit items, like canned or frozen jackfruit, have acquired fame as meat options in veggie lover and vegetarian consumes less calories. The flexibility of jackfruit's sinewy and substantial surface makes it a reasonable element for various culinary applications, from curries and stews to sandwiches and burgers.

In districts where jackfruit is a customary staple, handling techniques might incorporate drying or protecting the natural product for sometime later. Dried jackfruit, frequently alluded to as jackfruit chips, is a well known nibble in certain societies. The protection of jackfruit permits networks to partake in the organic product's flavors and wholesome advantages in any event, during periods when new jackfruit isn't promptly free.

The gathering of jackfruit, with its extraordinary difficulties and contemplations, embodies the crossing point of custom and advancement in horticulture. While customary techniques including manual apparatuses and shaft collecting stay common, mechanical headways have presented electric devices and mechanical gatherers to smooth out the cycle, especially in bigger scope activities. The decision of reaping strategies frequently relies upon elements like the size of development, accessible assets, and nearby rural practices.

Collecting jackfruit isn't just a mechanical errand yet a craftsmanship that requires a profound comprehension of the organic product's turn of events, maturing signals, and the subtleties of every assortment. The experience of prepared ranchers, frequently went down through ages, adds to the progress of the collect. As jackfruit keeps on catching worldwide consideration for its culinary flexibility and manageability, the craftsmanship and study of gathering stay essential to its excursion from the tree to the table.

5.4 Post-harvest handling and storage

Post-reap taking care of and stockpiling are basic stages in the excursion of natural products like jackfruit from the homestead to the shopper's table. Appropriate taking care of and stockpiling rehearses are fundamental to keep up with the natural product's quality, newness, and healthy benefit. On account of jackfruit, a tropical goliath with an unmistakable flavor and flexible culinary applications, these post-reap stages assume an essential part in guaranteeing that the natural product arrives at shoppers in ideal condition.

The most important phase in post-gather dealing with is the cautious vehicle of the reaped jackfruits from the plantation to capacity or handling offices. This stage expects meticulousness to forestall actual harm to the natural products, which could think twice about quality. Contingent upon the size of development and the vicinity of the plantation to business sectors or handling units, transportation strategies might shift.

For limited scope ranchers and nearby business sectors, physically moving jackfruits utilizing crates or holders is a typical practice. The natural products are organized cautiously to limit contact with hard surfaces, and padding materials might be utilized to forestall swelling or penetrates. In bigger business tasks, particularly those including significant distance transportation, specific compartments and bundling materials might be utilized to safeguard the jackfruits during travel.

After arriving at the capacity or handling office, the reaped jackfruits go through an arranging interaction. Arranging includes sorting the natural products in view of different measures like size, readiness, and quality. This step is urgent for guaranteeing that the natural products fulfill the guidelines expected for various market channels. Consistency in size and quality upgrades the attractiveness of the jackfruits and works with effective dissemination.

Now and again, handling offices might get jackfruits for change into esteem added items. The handling of jackfruit can take different structures, including canning, freezing, or drying out. These handled jackfruit items take care of different shopper needs, giving advantageous and flexible options in contrast to new jackfruit. Canned or frozen jackfruit, specifically, has acquired prevalence as a meat substitute in veggie lover and vegetarian consumes less calories.

For those dealing with new jackfruit, appropriate capacity is vital to keep up with the natural product's quality and broaden its time span of usability. Jackfruit is known for its transitory nature, and factors like temperature, mugginess, and ethylene responsiveness impact its post-reap conduct. Ethylene is a characteristic plant chemical that assumes a part in the maturing system, and a few natural products are delicate to its presence.

Temperature control is an essential part of post-collect capacity for jackfruit. The ideal stockpiling temperature for new jackfruit is regularly around 50°F to 55°F (10°C to 13°C). This temperature range dials back the aging system and diminishes the pace of ethylene creation, adding to the conservation of the organic product's quality. High temperatures can speed up aging and lead to overripeness, influencing both the surface and kind of the jackfruit.

Stickiness levels away offices likewise assume a part in keeping up with the newness of jackfruit. Jackfruit benefits from high stickiness, ordinarily somewhere in the range of 85% and 90%. Sufficient mugginess keeps the organic product from drying out and holds its normal dampness content. Dry circumstances can bring about a deficiency of bloat and adversely influence the surface of the jackfruit.

Ethylene awareness adds one more layer of intricacy to the capacity of jackfruit. While certain natural products are delicate to ethylene and can be unfavorably impacted by its presence, jackfruit is viewed as a low-ethylene-delivering organic product. Be that as it may, it is as yet critical to oversee ethylene openness during capacity, particularly on the off chance that jackfruit is put away close by other ethylene-delivering natural products. Isolating natural products with contrasting ethylene awarenesses can assist with safeguarding their singular characteristics.

Bundling likewise assumes a part in post-reap taking care of and stockpiling. Appropriate bundling safeguards jackfruits from outer factors like actual harm, pollutants, and vacillations in temperature and mugginess. Punctured plastic sacks or containers with great ventilation are usually utilized for new jackfruit, taking into consideration air flow while giving a level of security.

Notwithstanding temperature, dampness, and ethylene control, post-collect medicines, for example, waxing might be applied to jackfruits to make a defensive layer on the organic product's surface. This wax covering lessens dampness misfortune, limits the gamble of actual harm, and improves the natural product's general appearance. These medicines add to the visual allure of jackfruit and expand its market time span of usability.

In certain locales where jackfruit is a customary staple, post-gather taking care of includes safeguarding strategies to guarantee an all year supply. Drying is a typical practice, where jackfruit is cut and dried out for sometime later. Dried jackfruit, frequently alluded to as jackfruit chips, is a famous bite in certain societies. Safeguarding techniques broaden the accessibility of jackfruit as well as give an elective type of utilization.

Quality control measures are basic to post-reap taking care of, particularly in business settings. Visual assessments, arranging, and observing of temperature and dampness levels help recognize and resolve any issues that might emerge during capacity. Normal checks for readiness and indications of overripeness guarantee that main top notch jackfruits arrive at shoppers.

The term of capacity can shift in light of the expected market and dissemination channels. Momentary capacity might be adequate for jackfruits bound for nearby business sectors, where the time among reap and utilization is generally short. For jackfruits planned for longer-distance transportation or commodity markets, controlled environment capacity might be utilized to expand the natural product's time span of usability.

Controlled air capacity includes changing the degrees of oxygen, carbon dioxide, and stickiness inside the storage space to dial back the aging system. This technique is especially helpful for organic products with a high breath rate, like jackfruit. By establishing a climate that impedes the creation of ethylene and represses specific metabolic cycles, controlled environment capacity helps save the nature of jackfruit during expanded periods.

The advancement of transportation framework and worldwide exchange has worked with the product of tropical natural products like jackfruit to business sectors all over the planet. This development of market reach stresses the significance of successful post-gather dealing with and capacity practices to guarantee that jackfruit arrives at buyers in ideal condition, no matter what the geological distance.

Post-gather taking care of and stockpiling rehearses for jackfruit keep on developing with progressions in innovation and a developing comprehension of the organic product's novel qualities. Advancements in bundling materials, storerooms, and transportation strategies add to the protection of jackfruit quality from the homestead to the buyer.

The mix of maintainable practices, for example, the utilization of eco-accommodating bundling materials and energy-productive storage spaces, lines up with the more extensive objectives of decreasing natural effect.

All in all, post-reap dealing with and capacity are basic parts of the excursion of jackfruit from the plantation to the purchaser's table. These stages require a sensitive equilibrium of temperature, moistness, and ethylene control to keep up with the natural product's newness and quality. From conventional practices to current advancements, the methods utilized in post-reap dealing with and capacity add to the conservation of jackfruit's one of a kind flavors and wholesome advantages. As jackfruit keeps on acquiring notoriety universally, the refinement of post-gather practices will assume an essential part in fulfilling purchaser needs for superior grade, economical, and delightful natural product.

Dealing with and capacity are crucial stages in the rural excursion of organic products, including the tropical monster, jackfruit. The cautious administration of these post-reap stages is vital for safeguard the quality, newness, and dietary benefit of the natural product. Jackfruit, known for its particular flavor and adaptability in culinary applications, requires careful dealing with and capacity practices to guarantee it arrives at customers in ideal condition.

The underlying move toward post-collect taking care of is the vehicle of newly reaped jackfruits from the plantation to capacity or handling offices. This stage requests tender loving care to forestall actual harm to the organic products, a variable that could think twice about quality. The technique for transportation differs in view of the size of development and the closeness of the plantation to business sectors or handling units.

For limited scope ranchers and neighborhood markets, manual transportation of jackfruits utilizing bushels or holders is a typical practice. The natural products are organized cautiously to limit contact with hard surfaces, and padding materials might be utilized to forestall swelling or penetrates. Conversely, bigger business tasks, especially those including significant distance transportation, may use particular holders and bundling materials to defend the jackfruits during travel.

Upon landing in the capacity or handling office, the collected jackfruits go through a careful arranging process. Arranging includes sorting the organic products in view of different rules, including size, readiness, and quality. This step is essential for guaranteeing that the organic products fulfill the guidelines expected for various market channels. Consistency in size and quality upgrades the attractiveness of jackfruits and works with productive appropriation.

In certain cases, handling offices might get jackfruits for change into esteem added items. The handling of jackfruit can take different structures, including canning, freezing, or lack of hydration.

These handled jackfruit items take special care of different purchaser needs, giving helpful and flexible options in contrast to new jackfruit. Canned or frozen jackfruit, specifically, has acquired prominence as a meat substitute in veggie lover and vegetarian slims down.

For those taking care of new jackfruit, legitimate capacity is central to keep up with the natural product's quality and expand its time span of usability. Jackfruit is known for its short-lived nature, and factors like temperature, dampness, and ethylene awareness impact its post-collect way of behaving. Ethylene is a characteristic plant chemical that assumes a part in the maturing system, and a few organic products are delicate to its presence.

Temperature control is a urgent part of post-gather capacity for jackfruit. The ideal stockpiling temperature for new jackfruit is normally around 50°F to 55°F (10°C to 13°C). This temperature range dials back the aging system and diminishes the pace of ethylene creation, adding to the conservation of the organic product's quality. High temperatures can speed up aging and lead to overripeness, influencing both the surface and kind of the jackfruit.

Mugginess levels away offices likewise assume a part in keeping up with the newness of jackfruit. Jackfruit benefits from high mugginess, commonly somewhere in the range of 85% and 90%. Sufficient mugginess keeps the organic product from drying out and holds its normal dampness content. Dry circumstances can bring about a deficiency of bloat and adversely influence the surface of the jackfruit.

Ethylene responsiveness adds one more layer of intricacy to the capacity of jackfruit. While certain organic products are delicate to ethylene and can be unfavorably impacted by its presence, jackfruit is viewed as a low-ethylene-delivering natural product. Notwithstanding, it is as yet essential to oversee ethylene openness during capacity, particularly in the event that jackfruit is put away close by other ethylene-delivering natural products. Isolating organic products with contrasting ethylene awarenesses can assist with protecting their singular characteristics.

Bundling likewise assumes a vital part in post-gather taking care of and stockpiling. Legitimate bundling shields jackfruits from outer factors like actual harm, impurities, and changes in temperature and stickiness. Punctured plastic packs or boxes with great ventilation are generally utilized for new jackfruit, taking into consideration air flow while giving a level of security.

Notwithstanding temperature, moistness, and ethylene control, post-reap medicines, for example, waxing might be applied to jackfruits to make a defensive layer on the organic product's surface. This wax covering diminishes dampness misfortune, limits the gamble of actual harm, and improves the organic product's general appearance. These medicines add to the visual allure of jackfruit and broaden its market timeframe of realistic usability.

In certain locales where jackfruit is a conventional staple, post-gather dealing with includes protection techniques to guarantee an all year supply. Drying is a typical practice, where jackfruit is cut and dried out for sometime later. Dried jackfruit, frequently alluded to as jackfruit chips, is a well known nibble in certain societies. Safeguarding strategies broaden the accessibility of jackfruit as well as give an elective type of utilization.

Quality control measures are necessary to post-collect taking care of, particularly in business settings. Visual reviews, arranging, and observing of temperature and moistness levels help recognize and resolve any issues that might emerge during capacity. Ordinary checks for readiness and indications of overripeness guarantee that main excellent jackfruits arrive at buyers.

The span of capacity can change in light of the expected market and circulation channels. Transient capacity might be adequate for jackfruits bound for neighborhood markets, where the time among reap and utilization is somewhat concise. For jackfruits expected for longer-distance transportation or product markets, controlled air capacity might be utilized to expand the organic product's timeframe of realistic usability.

Controlled environment capacity includes changing the degrees of oxygen, carbon dioxide, and dampness inside the storage space to dial back the maturing system. This strategy is especially gainful for organic products with a high breath rate, like jackfruit. By establishing a climate that hinders the development of ethylene and restrains specific metabolic cycles, controlled air capacity helps protect the nature of jackfruit during broadened periods.

The advancement of transportation foundation and worldwide exchange has worked with the commodity of tropical organic products like jackfruit to business sectors all over the planet. This extension of market reach underscores the significance of powerful post-gather dealing with and capacity practices to guarantee that jackfruit arrives at buyers in ideal condition, no matter what the geological distance.

Post-gather taking care of and stockpiling rehearses for jackfruit keep on developing with headways in innovation and a developing comprehension of the organic product's extraordinary qualities. Developments in bundling materials, storerooms, and transportation strategies add to the protection of jackfruit quality from the homestead to the shopper. The joining of supportable practices, for example, the utilization of eco-accommodating bundling materials and energy-proficient storage spaces, lines up with the more extensive objectives of diminishing natural effect.

Chapter 6

Jackfruit in the Kitchen: Culinary Adventures

Jackfruit, a flexible and goliath tropical natural product, has been causing disturbances in the culinary world, charming gourmet specialists and food devotees with its exceptional flavor and substantial surface. Starting from Southwest India, the jackfruit tree (Artocarpus heterophyllus) bears the biggest product, all things considered, for certain examples gauging as much as 80 pounds. Its particular green, spiky outside conceals a mother lode of brilliant, stringy tissue and seeds, offering a plenty of culinary conceivable outcomes.

As of late, jackfruit has acquired fame as a plant-based meat substitute, especially among veggie lovers and vegetarians looking for options in contrast to customary protein sources. The natural product's unbiased taste and capacity to retain flavors make it a chameleon in the kitchen, adjusting to different foods and culinary methods. From flavorful dishes to sweet treats, jackfruit's flexibility exceeds all logical limitations.

One of the most widely recognized culinary purposes of jackfruit is as a meat substitute in flavorful dishes. The unripe, green jackfruit is great for this reason because of its impartial taste, which permits it to assume the kinds of the fixings it is cooked with. Jackfruit's stringy surface, when cooked, intently looks like pulled pork or destroyed chicken, going with it a famous decision for veggie lover and vegan variants of tacos, sandwiches, curries, and sautés.

To plan jackfruit for flavorful dishes, the natural product is normally depleted, washed, and afterward either bubbled or stewed until it becomes delicate. When cooked, the jackfruit can be effortlessly destroyed or pulled separated, making a substantial surface that ingests the kinds of the flavors and sauces it is cooked with. This flexibility makes jackfruit an adaptable element for making plant-based variants of exemplary dishes, for example, grill sandwiches, tacos al minister, and even bison "chicken" wraps.

Past its job as a meat substitute, jackfruit is a star fixing in different conventional dishes in its nations of beginning. In South and Southeast Asia, where jackfruit has been developed for quite a long time, it is highlighted in a wide cluster of recipes, both flavorful and sweet. In India, jackfruit is a critical part in the readiness of kathal ki biryani, a fragrant and tasty rice dish where the organic product is layered with sweet-smelling flavors and basmati rice.

Jackfruit seeds are likewise used in culinary manifestations, adding a nutty flavor and a dull surface to dishes. These seeds can be bubbled, simmered, or ground into a flour, offering a flexible element for both exquisite and sweet recipes. In Kerala, a state in South India, jackfruit seeds are many times utilized in curries and sautés, giving a special component to the dish.

As jackfruit keeps on catching the creative mind of gourmet specialists and home cooks the same, its presence reaches out past customary recipes. The organic product has turned into a material for culinary trial and error, rousing cooks to push the limits of flavor and surface. In the possession of imaginative cooks, jackfruit has tracked down its direction into startling dishes, from jackfruit sushi rolls to jackfruit frozen yogurt.

The sweet, ready rendition of jackfruit is a brilliant treat delighted in all alone or integrated into pastries. At the point when completely matured, the organic product changes from a green, bland surface to a sweet and fragrant one, with a taste suggestive of a blend of pineapple, mango, and banana. The brilliant yellow bulbs can be delighted in new, added to organic product servings of mixed greens, or mixed into smoothies for an explosion of regular pleasantness.

Jackfruit's regular pleasantness loans itself well to treats and heated merchandise. The ready organic product can be utilized to make sticks, jams, and jelly, catching its quintessence for satisfaction over time. In Indonesia, jackfruit is a famous fixing in a conventional pastry called es campur, a shaved ice treat highlighting a mixture of organic products, jams, and sweet syrups.

Notwithstanding its utilization in sweet dishes, jackfruit seeds can be ground into a flour and used in baking. This sans gluten flour adds a special nuttiness to bread, biscuits, and cakes, offering a nutritious option in contrast to conventional wheat flour. Jackfruit's development in the domain of baking exhibits its flexibility and the readiness of gourmet experts to investigate new and eccentric fixings.

Jackfruit's ascent in prominence has not exclusively been driven by its culinary adaptability yet in addition by its dietary profile. The natural product is a rich wellspring of dietary fiber, giving stomach related benefits, and is loaded with fundamental nutrients and minerals. It contains moderate measures of protein, making it a significant expansion to plant-based eats less. Moreover, jackfruit is low in calories and liberated from cholesterol and soaked fats, further upgrading its allure as a solid fixing.

The manageability of jackfruit development adds one more layer to its allure. The tree is strong and impervious to bothers, requiring negligible contribution to terms of pesticides and manures. Jackfruit trees likewise have a high return, delivering a huge amount of organic product that can take care of networks and add to food security. As familiarity with maintainable food decisions develops, jackfruit's capacity to flourish in different environments and its negligible natural effect position it as a feasible and eco-accommodating food source.

The excursion of jackfruit from a humble tropical organic product to a worldwide culinary sensation mirrors the developing scene of food inclinations and dietary decisions. Its flexibility, dietary advantages, and maintainability make it a convincing element for gourmet specialists, home cooks, and food fans the same. As culinary practices proceed to develop and embrace different impacts, jackfruit remains as an image of advancement and imagination in the kitchen.

All in all, jackfruit's culinary experiences reach out a long ways past its customary use in South and Southeast Asian foods. Its excursion from a terrace staple to a worldwide sensation grandstands the force of culinary development and the capacity of a solitary fixing to catch the creative mind of gourmet experts and food lovers. Whether utilized as a meat substitute in flavorful dishes or as a headliner in sweet treats, jackfruit's flexibility exceeds all logical limitations.

As we keep on investigating new flavors and fixings in the kitchen, jackfruit fills in as a sign of the rich embroidery of culinary customs and the vast potential outcomes that emerge when we embrace imagination and interest. From plant-based tacos to jackfruit-imbued treats, the culinary undertakings of jackfruit welcome us to grow our palates, challenge our predispositions, and appreciate the variety that the universe of food brings to the table. As we leave on our own culinary excursions, let jackfruit rouse us to find, try, and commend the enchanted that happens while we offer surprising elements of real value.

6.1 Diverse culinary uses of Jackfruit: From savory to sweet dishes

The culinary world is an embroidery woven with a bunch of flavors, surfaces, and fixings, each adding to the rich and various scene of worldwide cooking. Among the stars of this culinary troupe is the jackfruit, a flexible and colorful tropical organic product that has arisen as a culinary sensation. Its novel credits make it a sought-after fixing, offering a large number of conceivable outcomes in both flavorful and sweet dishes.

In the domain of flavorful manifestations, jackfruit becomes the overwhelming focus as a plant-based meat substitute, enthralling the taste buds of veggie lovers, vegetarians, and meat devotees the same. The unripe, green jackfruit, with its unbiased taste and stringy surface, fills in as an ideal material for engrossing the kinds of the dishes it graces. From pulled "pork" sandwiches to jackfruit curry, the culinary potential outcomes are essentially as immense as the creative mind of the cook.

The excursion of jackfruit from the tree to the table frequently includes a course of changing its crude, green state into a scrumptious and exquisite magnum opus. Regularly, the unripe jackfruit is depleted, flushed, and afterward cooked by one or the other bubbling or stewing until it accomplishes a delicate consistency. This interaction permits the natural product to be handily destroyed or pulled separated, copying the surface of destroyed meat. The outcome is a flexible fixing that can consistently coordinate into different culinary practices, offering a brutality free option in contrast to creature based proteins.

In the realm of tacos, jackfruit has turned into a praised filling, giving a substantial and fulfilling surface that matches well with different flavors and fixings. Whether prepared with conventional flavors for an exquisite kick or mixed with grill flavors for a smoky bend, jackfruit tacos have turned into a number one among those looking for plant-put together options without settling for less with respect to taste and fulfillment.

Another culinary experience including jackfruit unfurls in the domain of sandwiches. From pulled jackfruit sandwiches suggestive of pulled pork to jackfruit "chicken" wraps, this flexible natural product can ingest the substance of various cooking styles. The marriage of jackfruit and grill sauce makes an amicable ensemble of flavors, displaying how this tropical pearl can flawlessly coordinate into exemplary solace food.

Curries, a foundation of numerous South and Southeast Asian cooking styles, likewise welcome the presence of jackfruit. The capacity of the organic product to retain the intricate flavors and smells of curries makes it a convincing expansion to these customary dishes. Whether integrated into a hot Thai curry or a rich Indian masala, jackfruit loans its own special person to these tasty creations.

As culinary investigation has no limits, jackfruit tracks down its direction into unforeseen dishes, rethinking the limits of plant-based cooking. Jackfruit sushi rolls, with their blend of rice, ocean growth, and the organic product's remarkable surface, exhibit the natural product's versatility and its capacity to astonish and please sushi lovers. The marriage of conventional sushi components with the unforeseen bit of jackfruit exhibits the innovativeness and inventiveness that culinary experts bring to the kitchen.

While jackfruit's flavorful side takes the spotlight, its process doesn't end there. The organic product's change from a dull, green state to a sweet, brilliant readiness makes the way for a domain of sweet culinary potential outcomes. Ready jackfruit, with its inebriating fragrance and tropical pleasantness, turns into a magnificent expansion to sweets, sticks, and heated merchandise.

In its completely matured structure, jackfruit goes through a transformation, changing from an unbiased and stringy surface to a deliciously sweet and delicate state. The brilliant yellow bulbs of ready jackfruit, when delighted in new, offer a variety of flavors suggestive of pineapple, mango, and banana. This regular pleasantness makes ready jackfruit an ideal contender for consideration in natural product servings of mixed greens, smoothies, and other reviving treats.

The utilization of ready jackfruit reaches out past straightforward nibbling, tracking down its direction into the domain of sweets. The organic product's inborn pleasantness makes it an optimal element for jams, jams, and jam. The most common way of protecting ready jackfruit permits its flavors to be caught and delighted in consistently, offering a sample of tropical heaven even in the coldest months.

In Indonesian food, ready jackfruit is a headliner in a conventional treat known as es campur. This shaved ice treat includes a lively variety of natural products, jams, and sweet syrups, with ready jackfruit including its particular flavor and surface. The outcome is a reviving and outwardly engaging treat that exhibits the flexibility of jackfruit in the sweet culinary scene.

The bold soul of jackfruit doesn't stop at sweets; it reaches out into the domain of baking. Jackfruit seeds, when ground into a flour, offer a without gluten elective that adds a one of a kind nuttiness to bread, biscuits, and cakes. This imaginative utilization of jackfruit grandstands its versatility and the readiness of gourmet specialists to investigate unusual fixings in quest for different and tasty manifestations.

In districts like Kerala, South India, jackfruit seeds track down their direction into various culinary manifestations. These seeds, when bubbled or broiled, give a nutty flavor and a boring surface, offering a one of a kind component to curries and sautés. The mix of jackfruit seeds into appetizing dishes further epitomizes the organic product's adaptability and the creativity of culinary customs that use all aspects of the fixing.

Past its job as a culinary enjoyment, jackfruit flaunts a nourishing profile that adds to its allure. As a rich wellspring of dietary fiber, jackfruit adds to stomach related wellbeing and offers a feeling of satiety. Loaded with fundamental nutrients and minerals, including L-ascorbic acid, potassium, and dietary cell reinforcements, jackfruit gives a nutritious lift to the individuals who integrate it into their weight control plans.

Besides, jackfruit's moderate protein content makes it an important expansion to plant-based consumes less calories, offering an elective protein hotspot for those looking to decrease their dependence on creature items. As the interest for maintainable and plant-based choices keeps on rising, jackfruit's dietary advantages line up with the developing attention to wellbeing cognizant and ecologically cognizant food decisions.

The supportability of jackfruit development further improves its allure in a world progressively worried about the natural effect of food creation. Jackfruit trees are solid, impervious to bothers, and require negligible mediation as pesticides and manures. These attributes add to the general maintainability of jackfruit development, introducing it as an eco-accommodating food source that lines up with the standards of mindful and moral utilization.

The ascent of jackfruit as a worldwide culinary sensation is a demonstration of the steadily developing nature of food patterns and inclinations. From its beginnings in the tropical locales of Southwest India, jackfruit has ventured across mainlands, enamoring the taste buds of people looking for different and manageable culinary encounters. Its capacity to consistently coordinate into different foods, from the flavorful enjoyments of Southeast Asian curries to the sweet guilty pleasures of Western treats, positions jackfruit as an image of culinary combination and development.

As we investigate the different culinary purposes of jackfruit, we end up on an excursion that rises above topographical limits and social settings. The flexibility of jackfruit welcomes us to embrace new flavors, challenge our culinary predispositions, and praise the variety that the universe of food brings to the table. Whether utilized as an exquisite meat substitute or as a sweet expansion to pastries, jackfruit's culinary experiences move us to relish the extravagance of worldwide gastronomy and the vast potential outcomes that emerge when we open our palates to the miracles of different fixings.

6.2 Popular traditional and modern recipes

The universe of culinary enjoyments is a consistently extending domain where customary recipes and present day manifestations coincide, each offering an extraordinary excursion for the taste buds. This investigation envelops a different scope of flavors, methods, and social impacts that have formed the manner in which we experience food. From respected works of art went down through ages to imaginative dishes that push the limits of innovativeness, the culinary scene is an embroidery woven with the strings of custom and advancement.

Customary recipes act as a foundation of culinary legacy, saving the flavors and strategies that characterize a specific culture or district. These recipes are frequently permeated with history, sentimentality, and a feeling of character that rises above ages. In investigating customary dishes, we uncover an association with the previous, a connection that ties us to the culinary underlying foundations of our predecessors.

In the core of Italy, the ageless custom of creating pasta has persevered for quite a long time. From the fragile folds of ravioli to the long strands of spaghetti, pasta fills in as a material for a heap of flavors and sauces. Customary recipes like Spaghetti Bolognese, a rich and flavorful meat sauce matched with still somewhat firm pasta, exhibit the effortlessness and complexity of Italian cooking. The cautious equilibrium between fixings and the cunning readiness honor the culinary insight went down through ages.

Moving toward the east to Japan, the specialty of sushi-production has become inseparable from accuracy and tastefulness. Customary sushi recipes, like Nigiri and Sashimi, feature the magnificence of straightforwardness. Nigiri, little pieces of vinegared rice finished off with new fish, embody the Japanese obligation to quality fixings and fastidious show. In the mean time, Sashimi praises the immaculateness of crude fish, masterfully cut and presented with negligible enhancement, permitting the normal flavors to become the overwhelming focus.

In the dynamic woven artwork of Indian cooking, recipes like Chicken Tikka Masala grandstand the intricacy and profundity of flavors that have made this food darling around the world. Marinated and barbecued chicken is encompassed in a tasty tomato-based curry sauce, making a dish that adjusts intensity, pleasantness, and lavishness. This famous recipe is a demonstration of the culinary masterfulness tracked down in customary Indian kitchens, where flavors are used like paintbrushes, making magnum opuses of flavor.

Conventional recipes frequently reach out past the exquisite domain into the domain of desserts, where sweets become a material for culinary articulation. In France, the sensitive layers of an exemplary Mille-feuille, or Napoleon, uncover the artfulness of French baked good making. Puff baked good is fastidiously layered with cake cream, making a treat that encapsulates the marriage of straightforwardness and complexity, a sign of French patisserie.

As we enjoy the extravagance of customary recipes, recognizing the unique idea of the culinary world is fundamental. The advancement of gastronomy ceaselessly acquaints us with new fixings, methods, and flavor mixes. Present day recipes, brought into the world from a feeling of development and trial and error, welcome us to leave on culinary experiences that push the limits of what is conceivable in the kitchen.

In the domain of current cooking, combination dishes have arisen as a demonstration of the interconnectedness of worldwide flavors. The marriage of different culinary practices leads to manifestations like Korean Tacos, where the strong and fiery kinds of Korean grill meet the

natural hug of a taco shell. This combination of Korean and Mexican components brings about an amicable mix of sweet, flavorful, and umami, displaying the imagination that emerges when culinary limits are liquid.

Imaginative cooking strategies likewise assume a significant part in current recipes, lifting the eating experience higher than ever. Atomic gastronomy, for instance, presents unusual strategies, for example, sous-vide cooking, frothing, and spherification. Dishes like Nitro-Fried Eggs, where eggs are cooked utilizing fluid nitrogen to accomplish a smooth surface, represent the groundbreaking force of current methods in the kitchen. These vanguard approaches challenge our view of recognizable fixings, opening ways to previously unheard-of conceivable outcomes.

Plant-based cooking has flooded to the very front of present day culinary patterns, driven by a developing familiarity with supportability and a longing for better eating. Current recipes embrace plant-based fixings in imaginative ways, making dishes that rival their creature based partners. The ascent of the Unthinkable Burger, a plant-based patty that copies the taste and surface of hamburger, features the creativity of present day culinary science in reclassifying the conceivable outcomes of veggie lover and vegetarian food.

In the domain of sweets, current baked good gourmet experts explore different avenues regarding vanguard strategies and unforeseen flavor mixes. Dismantled sweets, where conventional treats are reconsidered and introduced in an outwardly striking way, have turned into a sign of current patisserie. These manifestations, for example, a dismantled Tiramisu with coffee gel circles and mascarpone froth, embody the imaginative and exploratory nature of contemporary sweet making.

The incorporation of innovation into the culinary world has additionally led to present day recipes that embrace the computerized age. Virtual cooking classes, online recipe stages, and savvy kitchen machines have become vital pieces of the advanced culinary experience. With the tap of a screen, home cooks can get to a gold mine of recipes, cooking tips, and culinary motivation from around the globe. The computerized scene has democratized culinary information, permitting people to investigate assorted recipes and methods from the solace of their kitchens.

In the combination of conventional and present day recipes, we witness a powerful exchange that mirrors the steadily changing nature of culinary culture. Gourmet experts and home cooks the same draw motivation from both the past and the present, mixing revered methods with contemporary imagination. The outcome is a culinary mosaic that praises the variety of flavors, surfaces, and social impacts that characterize our worldwide gastronomic scene.

As we explore this culinary excursion, it's obvious that the differentiation among customary and present day recipes is definitely not an inflexible limit however a liquid continuum. Customary recipes, with their profound roots in social legacy, give an establishment to culinary investigation. In the mean time, current recipes, with their soul of development, drive us into strange domains, welcoming us to rethink the potential outcomes of what can be accomplished in the kitchen.

All in all, the universe of culinary pleasures is a dynamic and steadily developing embroidery woven with the strings of custom and innovation. Conventional recipes act as mainstays of culinary legacy, protecting the flavors and procedures that characterize social personalities. These works of art, whether Italian pasta, Japanese sushi, Indian curries, or French cakes, associate us to the culinary insight of previous eras.

Then again, current recipes push the limits of imagination and development, acquainting us with new fixings, procedures, and flavor blends. The combination of worldwide flavors, the hug of plant-based cooking, and the joining of innovation into the kitchen epitomize the extraordinary idea of present day gastronomy. In the exchange among custom and advancement, we track down a rich and different culinary scene that welcomes us to investigate, trial, and enjoy the limitless potential outcomes that unfurl in the realm of food.

6.3 Nutritional aspects of Jackfruit-based meals

The culinary world is steadily developing, and with the rising spotlight on wellbeing and manageability, elective fixings are acquiring unmistakable quality. Jackfruit, a huge and flexible tropical natural product, has ventured into the spotlight, for its culinary allure as well as for its eminent wholesome advantages. As a plant-based fixing, jackfruit has earned consideration for giving a nutritious and economical option in various meals potential.

One of the critical nourishing parts of jackfruit is its low-calorie content, going with it a great decision for those hoping to keep a solid weight. The organic product is normally low in fat, with immaterial measures of immersed fat, and its calorie content is essentially gotten from sugars. This trademark makes jackfruit a brilliant choice for those trying to integrate supplement thick food varieties into their eating routine without inordinate calorie admission.

Jackfruit's great dietary profile reaches out to its fiber content. Fiber is a fundamental part of a solid eating regimen, supporting processing, advancing a sensation of completion, and adding to generally speaking stomach wellbeing. The sinewy idea of jackfruit, particularly in its unripe state, gives a fantastic surface in flavorful dishes while offering a critical portion of dietary fiber. This quality makes jackfruit an important expansion to feasts pointed toward supporting stomach related prosperity.

Notwithstanding its fiber content, jackfruit stands apart as a wellspring of different fundamental nutrients and minerals. The natural product is plentiful in L-ascorbic acid, a cancer prevention agent that upholds the resistant framework, advances skin wellbeing, and helps in the retention of iron from plant-based sources. Jackfruit likewise contains potassium, a mineral urgent for keeping up with legitimate liquid equilibrium, managing circulatory strain, and supporting heart wellbeing.

Jackfruit's moderate protein content is another imperative perspective, especially for those looking for plant-based protein options. While jackfruit doesn't match the protein levels found in creature items, its protein content is similar to other plant-based sources. Protein is fundamental for muscle fix, safe capability, and generally cell wellbeing, making jackfruit a significant expansion to veggie lover and vegetarian counts calories.

The flexibility of jackfruit in the kitchen permits it to act as a meat substitute in different dishes, taking special care of people embracing a plant-based way of life. Whether utilized in tacos, pan-sears, curries, or sandwiches, jackfruit's capacity to impersonate the surface of destroyed meat gives a delightful and protein-rich other option. This adaptability opens up additional opportunities for people hoping to lessen their meat utilization without settling on flavor and sustenance.

The idea of complete proteins is frequently connected with creature items, as they commonly contain all fundamental amino acids in adequate sums. While individual plant-based food varieties might miss the mark on amino acids, joining an assortment of plant-based sources, like vegetables, grains, and vegetables, can make a total and adjusted amino corrosive profile. Jackfruit, when integrated into a different and balanced plant-based diet, adds to the general amino corrosive admission.

For those zeroed in on weight the board or glucose control, the glycemic record (GI) of food sources turns into a pivotal thought. The GI estimates how rapidly a food raises glucose levels. Low-GI food sources are ingested all the more leisurely, giving a progressive arrival of energy and advancing satiety. Jackfruit, with its somewhat low glycemic record, can be a reasonable decision for people looking for food varieties that add to stable glucose levels.

In addition, the healthful advantages of jackfruit reach out to its micronutrient content. The natural product contains different nutrients and minerals, including vitamin A, vitamin B6, niacin, riboflavin, and manganese. These micronutrients assume fundamental parts in keeping up with skin wellbeing, supporting energy digestion, and adding to generally speaking prosperity. Remembering jackfruit for a decent eating regimen can in this manner add to meeting day to day micronutrient necessities.

The presence of cancer prevention agents in jackfruit adds one more layer to its healthy benefit. Cancer prevention agents assist with combatting oxidative pressure in the body, which is connected to maturing and different constant sicknesses. The different scope of cell reinforcements found in jackfruit incorporates carotenoids, flavonoids, and phenolic compounds. These cell reinforcements add to the organic product's dynamic tone and, when consumed, support the body's safeguard against free extremists.

While the wholesome advantages of jackfruit are significant, taking into account its culinary preparation is fundamental. The technique for cooking and the fixings utilized in jackfruit-based dinners can impact the by and large nourishing substance of the dish. For example, selecting better cooking strategies like baking, barbecuing, or steaming can safeguard the nourishing honesty of the natural product, while searing or inordinate utilization of oils might add pointless calories and fats.

Similarly as with any dietary thought, individual nourishing requirements and inclinations change. A few people might decide to integrate jackfruit as an essential protein source, while others might see it as a correlative expansion to a different exhibit of plant-based food sources. The adaptability of jackfruit in the kitchen considers imaginative and nutritious feast choices that take care of a scope of dietary inclinations and wellbeing objectives.

With regards to supportability, another perspective acquiring noticeable quality in healthful conversations, jackfruit sparkles as a low-influence food source. The jackfruit tree is tough, versatile, and requires insignificant information sources like pesticides and manures. Its capacity to flourish in different environments adds to its true capacity as a practical food source that can uphold food security drives worldwide.

The excursion of jackfruit from a conventional staple in South and Southeast Asian cooking styles to a worldwide culinary sensation lines up with the developing scene of dietary decisions. As additional people investigate plant-based eats less, decrease their meat utilization, and look for maintainable food options, jackfruit has arisen as an image of development in the kitchen.

All in all, the healthful parts of jackfruit make it a convincing expansion to a reasonable and plant-centered diet. Its low-calorie content, fiber lavishness, moderate protein levels, and cluster of fundamental nutrients and minerals add to its allure as a flexible and nutritious fixing. As dietary examples proceed to broaden and people look for economical and wellbeing cognizant decisions, jackfruit's presence in the culinary world is probably going to develop, offering a tasty and supplement stuffed choice for those embracing the advantages of plant-based eating.

6.4 Exploring the global popularity of Jackfruit in various cuisines

The worldwide culinary scene is an energetic embroidery woven with different flavors, surfaces, and fixings. One such fixing that has navigated borders and acquired far and wide fame is jackfruit. Local to South and Southeast Asia, jackfruit has risen above its territorial beginnings to turn into a worldwide sensation, tracking down its direction into a bunch of foods all over the planet. The excursion of jackfruit from a conventional staple to a culinary peculiarity is a demonstration of its flexibility, versatility, and the steadily growing palates of food devotees.

In its nations of beginning, especially in India and Bangladesh, jackfruit has been a dietary pillar for quite a long time. The natural product, referred to locally as "kathal" in Hindi, is used in various dishes, both flavorful and sweet. In South Indian cooking, jackfruit is a vital fixing in dishes like "kathal biryani," where the unripe natural product is layered with fragrant rice and sweet-smelling flavors, making a delightful and fulfilling feast. The sinewy surface of unripe jackfruit loans itself well to curries, sautés, and customary dishes that structure the culinary woven artwork of the area.

In Southeast Asia, jackfruit is embraced along these lines, with nations like Indonesia, Malaysia, and the Philippines integrating it into their culinary customs. In Indonesia, jackfruit is a headliner in the conventional treat "kolak," a sweet and flavored coconut milk soup highlighting jackfruit, bananas, and different natural products. The flexibility of jackfruit is clear in its capacity to consistently progress from appetizing dishes to sweet treats, adjusting to the assorted flavor profiles of Southeast Asian food.

As the culinary world turns out to be progressively interconnected, jackfruit has left on a worldwide excursion, catching the consideration of gourmet experts, home cooks, and food devotees around the world. One of the variables adding to its worldwide prominence is its capacity to act as a meat substitute in exquisite dishes. The unripe, green jackfruit, with its nonpartisan taste and sinewy surface, has acquired praise as a plant-based option in contrast to destroyed meat. Its flexibility permits it to retain the kinds of the dishes it is cooked with, making it a chameleon in the kitchen.

In Western cooking styles, especially in the US and Europe, jackfruit has found a specialty as a meat substitute in veggie lover and vegetarian dishes. Jackfruit tacos, sandwiches, and curries have become famous options for those looking for plant-based other options. The ascent of plant-based eating and the interest for imaginative meat substitutes have pushed jackfruit into the spotlight, with its capacity to impersonate the surface of pulled pork or destroyed chicken making it a sought-after fixing in different exquisite dishes.

In the domain of road food, jackfruit has likewise had a huge effect. Food trucks and stylish diners all over the planet have embraced jackfruit as a headliner in imaginative and tasty dishes. Jackfruit sliders, grill sandwiches, and even jackfruit-based "carnitas" have become staples in road food scenes, interesting to a different crowd with a propensity for strong and gutsy flavors.

Jackfruit's flexibility stretches out to job in worldwide cooking styles have generally been meat-driven. In Mexican food, jackfruit has found a spot in dishes like "tacos al minister," where the natural product's surface and capacity to retain flavors sparkle close by conventional flavors and flavors. The combination of jackfruit with Mexican flavors embodies the flexibility of the leafy foods ability to lift exemplary dishes with a plant-based curve.

The ascent of jackfruit in worldwide cooking isn't restricted to flavorful dishes; it has likewise transformed the domain of pastries. In Western nations, especially in the US, jackfruit has been integrated into sweet treats and prepared products. Jackfruit frozen yogurt, smoothies, and treats including the ready, sweet adaptation of the organic product have become famous options for those looking for inventive and tropical-enhanced guilty pleasures.

The culinary innovativeness encompassing jackfruit isn't bound to customary recipes. Gourmet experts and home cooks the same have embraced the natural product as a material for trial and error, prompting startling and superb culinary developments. Jackfruit sushi rolls, for instance, feature the natural product's capacity to supplement the customary components of sushi, offering an extraordinary bend on a dearest Japanese dish. The combination of worldwide flavors with the versatility of jackfruit mirrors the unique idea of contemporary culinary investigation.

In Australia, where the food scene is impacted by different social customs, jackfruit has tracked down its direction into different dishes, adding a tropical energy to the culinary scene. From jackfruit burgers to Thai-motivated jackfruit servings of mixed greens, the organic product's flexibility is embraced in both easygoing and upscale feasting foundations. The acknowledgment of jackfruit in various culinary settings highlights its capacity to rise above social limits and become a worldwide culinary peculiarity.

The flood in prominence of jackfruit has not slipped through the cracks by the food business. Jackfruit-based items, including canned jackfruit, jackfruit snacks, and pre-bundled jackfruit dinners, have become all the more promptly accessible in general stores and supermarkets. This openness has additionally energized the reception of jackfruit into standard culinary culture, making it a helpful choice for home cooks and shoppers anxious to investigate new and imaginative fixings.

The nourishing parts of jackfruit, including its low-calorie content, fiber wealth, and moderate protein levels, line up with contemporary dietary inclinations zeroed in on wellbeing and health. As people become more aware of their food decisions and look for plant-based other options, jackfruit arises as a nutritious choice that fulfills the taste buds as well as adds to a balanced and adjusted diet.

Past its culinary allure, the worldwide fame of jackfruit has suggestions for supportability and natural awareness. The jackfruit tree is tough, strong, and requires negligible contributions to terms of pesticides and manures. Its capacity to flourish in different environments and give a high return positions it as a maintainable food source. As discussions around manageable eating build up some decent forward momentum, jackfruit's capability to add to eco-accommodating and plant-based consumes less calories turns out to be progressively significant.

The worldwide ubiquity of jackfruit is a demonstration of the developing idea of culinary inclinations and the readiness of people to embrace different and creative fixings. Jackfruit's excursion from a customary fixing in South and Southeast Asian cooking styles to a worldwide culinary peculiarity mirrors the interconnectedness of the world through food. As the limits among provincial and worldwide foods obscure, jackfruit remains as an image of culinary combination, versatility, and the common delight of investigating new flavors from around the world.

All in all, the worldwide notoriety of jackfruit is a culinary peculiarity that rises above social lines and mirrors the unique idea of contemporary gastronomy. From its conventional roots in South and Southeast Asia to its reconciliation into different worldwide cooking styles, jackfruit has turned into an image of development and flexibility in the kitchen. As the world keeps on investigating the potential outcomes of plant-based eating, supportable fixings, and worldwide culinary combination, jackfruit's presence on the worldwide stage is probably going to develop, offering a sample of tropical joy to food devotees all over the planet.

Jackfruit, the flexible and monster tropical natural product, has found its direction into different cooking styles across the globe, dazzling the taste buds of individuals from various societies. Local to South and Southeast Asia, jackfruit has been a culinary staple in nations like India and Bangladesh for a really long time. In these locales, both the ready and unripe variants of the organic product are used in a variety of conventional dishes, displaying its flexibility and adaptability.

In South Indian food, unripe jackfruit becomes the dominant focal point in exquisite manifestations like "kathal biryani," a fragrant and delightful rice dish layered with flavors and basmati rice. The stringy surface of unripe jackfruit permits it to ingest the rich kinds of the flavors, making a generous and fulfilling dinner. Also, jackfruit curry and pan-sears are normal arrangements, exhibiting the organic product's consistent mix into the different culinary embroidered artwork of South India.

Southeast Asian nations, including Indonesia, Malaysia, and the Philippines, have embraced jackfruit as a culinary fortune. In Indonesia, jackfruit is highlighted in the customary pastry "kolak," a sweet coconut milk soup enhanced with the organic product's regular pleasantness.

The flexibility of jackfruit is obvious in its progress from exquisite to sweet dishes, mirroring its capacity to fit with an assortment of flavor profiles.

The worldwide notoriety of jackfruit has flooded in Western nations, where it has turned into a praised fixing in both veggie lover and vegetarian cooking styles. The unripe, green jackfruit's sinewy surface makes it an optimal substitute for destroyed meat, and it has turned into a headliner in dishes like jackfruit tacos, sandwiches, and curries. Its nonpartisan taste permits it to ingest the kinds of flavors and sauces, giving a delightful and substantial option for those looking for plant-based choices.

The combination of jackfruit with conventional Mexican flavors is exemplified in dishes like "tacos al minister," where the natural product's surface supplements the strong flavors and flavors of the exemplary taco filling. The capacity of jackfruit to impersonate the surface of pulled pork or destroyed chicken has made it a sought-after fixing in the realm of plant-based cooking.

Jackfruit has likewise left an imprint in Western sweets and heated merchandise. In the US and Europe, ready jackfruit has been integrated into sweet deals with like frozen yogurt, smoothies, and treats. Its tropical pleasantness adds a one of a kind and outlandish component to conventional Western treats, exhibiting its flexibility in both sweet and exquisite culinary domains.

Australia, with its different culinary scene affected by different social practices, has embraced jackfruit in imaginative and tasty ways. From jackfruit burgers to Thai-roused servings of mixed greens, the organic product has turned into a staple in both relaxed and upscale eating foundations. The combination of jackfruit with different worldwide flavors mirrors its capacity to rise above social limits and become a worldwide culinary peculiarity.

The ascent of jackfruit in the culinary world isn't restricted to customary recipes; gourmet experts and home cooks the same have involved the natural product as a material for trial and error. Jackfruit sushi rolls, for example, grandstand its capacity to supplement customary components of Japanese cooking, offering a novel wind on a cherished dish. The combination of worldwide flavors with the versatility of jackfruit mirrors the powerful idea of contemporary culinary investigation.

Past its culinary allure, the dietary parts of jackfruit add to its ubiquity. With its low-calorie content, fiber extravagance, and moderate protein levels, jackfruit lines up with contemporary dietary inclinations zeroed in on wellbeing and health. As people become more aware of their food decisions and look for plant-based other options, jackfruit arises as a nutritious choice that fulfills the taste buds as well as adds to a balanced and adjusted diet.

The supportability of jackfruit development adds one more layer to its allure. The jackfruit tree is strong, tough, and requires negligible information sources like pesticides and composts. Its capacity to flourish in different environments and give a high return positions it as an economical food source. As discussions around reasonable eating get some decent momentum, jackfruit's capability to add to eco-accommodating and plant-based abstains from food turns out to be progressively applicable.

All in all, jackfruit's excursion from a customary fixing in South and Southeast Asian cooking styles to a worldwide culinary peculiarity is a demonstration of its flexibility, adaptability, and allure in different culinary practices. From flavorful curries in India to plant-based tacos in the US, jackfruit has demonstrated to be a dynamic and energizing expansion to the universe of gastronomy. Its capacity to flawlessly progress among sweet and flavorful dishes, combined with its wholesome advantages and manageability, positions jackfruit as a culinary diamond that keeps on dazzling the taste buds of food lovers all over the planet.

Chapter 7

Beyond the Table: Jackfruit in Sustainable Agriculture

The sun sets over the rich scene, projecting a warm gleam on the fields that stretch as may be obvious. In this agrarian perfect world, a quiet transformation is occurring — one that goes past the recognizable harvests and customary cultivating strategies. It's an account of strength, variety, and maintainability, with the unpretentious jackfruit at its heart.

Jackfruit, logically known as Artocarpus heterophyllus, is a tropical tree natural product local to southwest India. Adored for its colossal size and particular flavor, this adaptable natural product has tracked down its direction into the hearts and kitchens of individuals all over the planet. In any case, its importance goes past its culinary allure; jackfruit is arising as a vital participant in maintainable farming, adding to food security, ecological protection, and monetary turn of events.

At the core of jackfruit's supportability is its wonderful flexibility. Flourishing in different environments and soil conditions, jackfruit trees require negligible support, making them strong notwithstanding environmental change and flighty weather conditions. As worldwide temperatures increase and climate occasions become more limit, the capacity of yields to adjust becomes critical for food security. Jackfruit's capacity to endure testing conditions positions it as a versatile and dependable wellspring of sustenance even with an evolving environment.

Besides, jackfruit is a help for biodiversity. The tree's enormous overhang gives conceal and a living space to different types of birds, bugs, and microorganisms. In a period where monoculture rules numerous rural scenes, jackfruit stands apart as a hero of biodiversity, making environments that help a wide exhibit of vegetation. As customary horticultural practices give way to modern cultivating, the conservation of biodiversity becomes principal for keeping up with the wellbeing of our planet.

The financial advantages of jackfruit development are similarly convincing. Not at all like some high-support crops that request broad consideration and information, jackfruit trees require negligible consideration once settled. This makes them an alluring choice for limited scope ranchers with restricted assets. The low-input, high-yield nature of jackfruit cultivating can possibly inspire networks by giving a supportable kind of revenue and business valuable open doors.

Notwithstanding its versatility and monetary benefits, jackfruit adds to manageable horticulture through its part in soil preservation. The tree's broad underground root growth forestalls soil disintegration, a basic issue in numerous locales where traditional cultivating has prompted the corruption of arable land. By securing the dirt and advancing water maintenance, jackfruit trees assume an essential part in keeping up with the wellbeing and richness of rural scenes.

As the sun ascends on one more day in the jackfruit plantations, the tale of feasible farming unfurls. A story challenges customary ideas of cultivating and offers a brief look into a future where flexibility, variety, and ecological stewardship are at the very front of rural practices. The excursion from seed to table is a demonstration of the interconnectedness of environments and the potential for supportable answers for address the squeezing difficulties within recent memory.

Jackfruit's process starts with the planting of seeds — small vessels of potential that hold the commitment of a strong and reasonable future. As the saplings rise up out of the dirt, they mark the start of a groundbreaking cycle that rises above the limits of customary farming. The youthful trees are solid, adjusting to a scope of environments from damp tropical districts to drier subtropical zones. This versatility is a critical figure jackfruit's developing prevalence as an economical harvest.

The development of jackfruit trees is a scene in itself. The branches stretch out every which way, making a rambling covering that gives shade to the vegetation underneath. This thick foliage protects the ground as well as makes a microclimate helpful for the development of different plant species. It's a living demonstration of the harmonious connection between jackfruit trees and the climate, a relationship that goes past simple development.

Chasing maintainability, jackfruit remains as an image of agroecology — a comprehensive way to deal with cultivating that underlines the reconciliation of environmental standards into rural frameworks. By tackling the force of normal cycles and biodiversity, jackfruit plantations become something other than fields of development; they advance into lively biological systems that help life in the entirety of its structures. Birds find asylum in the branches, bugs fertilize the blooms, and microorganisms enhance the dirt — all cooperating as one.

The flexibility of jackfruit stretches out past its versatility to various environments; it likewise appears in the natural product itself. Jackfruit is extraordinary in its organization, offering both a bland part like potatoes and a sweet, fragrant tissue suggestive of tropical natural products. This duality makes it a culinary chameleon, equipped for taking on various jobs in the kitchen. From exquisite curries and stews to sweet treats and tidbits, jackfruit has procured its put on tables all over the planet.

In the domain of reasonable horticulture, the culinary allure of jackfruit assumes a critical part. As attention to natural issues develops, customers are looking for choices that line up with their qualities. Jackfruit's capacity to act as a meat substitute has gathered consideration, particularly with regards to the developing interest for plant-based consumes less calories. The sinewy surface of unripe jackfruit intently looks like that of meat, settling on it a well known decision for veggie lover and vegetarian dishes.

The ascent of jackfruit as a meat elective isn't just a culinary pattern; it's a reaction to the natural effect of traditional domesticated animals cultivating. The creation of meat, particularly hamburger, is related with deforestation, ozone harming substance emanations, and asset concentrated rehearses. Jackfruit offers a manageable elective that requires less assets, produces less emanations, and diminishes the biological impression related with meat utilization.

Past the natural advantages, jackfruit's job in plant-based eats less carbs adds to worldwide food security. As the total populace keeps on developing, the interest for food is putting phenomenal tension on farming frameworks. Traditional meat creation is asset serious and frequently wasteful as far as changing over feed into consumable protein. Jackfruit presents a potential chance to address this test by giving a nutritious and flexible elective that can be developed with more prominent productivity.

The financial ramifications of jackfruit as a meat elective are significant. For ranchers, the development of jackfruit opens new business sectors and amazing open doors. As the interest for plant-based items rises, the worth of jackfruit as a money crop increments. This monetary motivation benefits individual ranchers as well as adds to the improvement of reasonable farming practices for a bigger scope.

The excursion of jackfruit from ranch to table is a story of interconnectedness — a snare of connections that stretches out from the underlying foundations of the tree to the customers partaking in a dinner. As the natural product arrives at development, it goes through a change that denotes the start of its excursion past the plantation. Reaping jackfruit requires expertise and accuracy, as the natural products can gauge as much as 80 pounds each. The cycle is a fragile dance between the rancher and nature, a joint effort that comes full circle in the abundance of the collect.

When gathered, the jackfruit goes through a fastidious readiness interaction to make it reasonable for utilization. The huge organic products are cut open, uncovering the meaty bulbs settled inside. The seeds, frequently disposed of, are a nutritious part that can be cooked or bubbled, offering an economical bite that supplements the culinary flexibility of the natural product. The bulbs, with their unmistakable surface and flavor, become the point of convergence of a large number of dishes.

In the kitchen, jackfruit assumes the job of a culinary chameleon. In its unripe state, it retains the kinds of the dishes it is cooked with, making it an optimal contender for exquisite arrangements. Jackfruit curry, stew, and tacos are only a couple of instances of the exquisite pleasures that feature its capacity to impersonate the surface of meat. As a sweet organic product, ready jackfruit fits treats, smoothies, and jams, adding a tropical curve to conventional recipes.

The culinary excursion of jackfruit stretches out past conventional dishes, tracking down way into inventive and imaginative recipes push the limits of gastronomy. From jackfruit burgers that rival their meat partners to jackfruit frozen yogurt that amuses the faculties, culinary specialists and home cooks the same are finding the vast potential outcomes that this modest organic product offers. In this culinary investigation, jackfruit fulfills the sense of taste as well as difficulties assumptions about food and maintainability.

As shoppers embrace jackfruit as a culinary joy, its part in manageable horticulture turns out to be significantly more articulated. The interest for jackfruit as a meat elective makes a market-driven impetus for ranchers to develop this flexible yield. This monetary open door, thusly, adds to the far reaching reception of reasonable cultivating rehearses. The combination of jackfruit into farming scenes turns into an impetus for change, cultivating flexibility and variety notwithstanding ecological difficulties.

The excursion of jackfruit doesn't end at the table; it reaches out into the domain of waste decrease and round economies. The side-effects of jackfruit handling, like strips and seeds, hold undiscovered possibility for different applications. Jackfruit strips, wealthy in fiber and supplements, can be utilized to make biodegradable bundling materials, diminishing the natural effect of single-use plastics. Jackfruit seeds, frequently disposed of, can be ground into flour or handled to separate oil, enhancing what was once viewed as waste.

In the mission for supportability, the usage of jackfruit results represents the standards of a round economy — a framework where assets are utilized proficiently, squander is limited, and items are planned in light of end-of-life contemplations. By tackling the maximum capacity of jackfruit, from organic product to strip to seed, a shut circle framework arises, diminishing the natural impression of the whole worth chain.

The ecological advantages of jackfruit don't stop at squander decrease; they reach out to soil wellbeing and carbon sequestration. Jackfruit trees, with their broad underground roots, assume a urgent part in forestalling soil disintegration and keeping up with soil richness. The natural matter from fallen leaves and rotting plant material adds to the enhancement of the dirt, making a maintainable pattern of supplement cycling.

Also, the carbon sequestration capability of jackfruit trees adds one more layer to their part in relieving environmental change. As trees develop, they retain carbon dioxide from the environment, putting away carbon in their biomass and the dirt.

In a period where deforestation and land corruption contribute altogether to ozone harming substance discharges, the afforestation and reforestation endeavors related with jackfruit development add to the worldwide battle against environmental change.

The excursion of jackfruit from seed to table, from homestead to kitchen, is a story of interconnectedness and reliance. It features the complicated dance among people and nature, where maintainable farming isn't simply an idea yet a lifestyle. The tale of jackfruit challenges the customary stories of food creation and utilization, offering a brief look into a future where strength, variety, and ecological stewardship are vital.

As the sun sets over the jackfruit plantations, creating long shaded areas on the scene, the excursion proceeds. An excursion rises above lines and societies, joining individuals in the common quest for a supportable and sustained future. Past the table, past the plantation, jackfruit remains as an image of probability — a demonstration of the extraordinary force of farming when directed by standards of supportability and environmental congruity. In the steadily developing story of our relationship with the land, jackfruit is an encouraging sign, guiding the way to a future where the underlying foundations of strength run profound, and the products of supportability are shared by all.

7.1 Jackfruit as a sustainable crop: Benefits for the environment

Jackfruit, a tropical tree organic product local to southwest India, is earning respect for its culinary flexibility as well as for its true capacity as a reasonable yield with various ecological advantages. Despite environmental change and the requirement for versatile farming practices, jackfruit arises as a promising arrangement because of its flexibility to different environments and negligible support prerequisites. This versatility positions jackfruit as a powerful wellspring of nourishment that can endure the difficulties of an evolving environment, adding to food security on a worldwide scale.

One of the critical natural benefits of jackfruit development lies in its capacity to advance biodiversity. The huge covering of jackfruit trees gives shade and environment to different types of birds, bugs, and microorganisms. In a rural scene frequently overwhelmed by monoculture, jackfruit plantations stand apart as shelters for biodiversity, encouraging environments that help a wide cluster of vegetation. As customary cultivating rehearses give way to modern farming, the conservation of biodiversity becomes fundamental for keeping up with the biological equilibrium of our planet.

The monetary advantages of jackfruit as a supportable yield are similarly imperative. Dissimilar to high-upkeep crops that request broad consideration and info, jackfruit trees are somewhat low-support once settled. This trademark makes them an alluring choice for limited scope ranchers with restricted assets, offering a manageable kind of revenue and business open doors. The monetary reasonability of jackfruit development adds to the strength of nearby networks, especially in areas where conventional cultivating faces difficulties from environment changeability and financial vulnerabilities.

Besides, jackfruit assumes a huge part in soil protection — a basic part of supportable horticulture. The broad underground root growth of jackfruit trees forestalls soil disintegration, a typical issue in regions where customary cultivating rehearses have prompted the debasement of arable land. By mooring the dirt and advancing water maintenance, jackfruit trees add to keeping up with the wellbeing and fruitfulness of horticultural scenes. In reality as we know it where soil corruption is a developing concern, the dirt protection advantages of jackfruit make it an important resource in economical cultivating rehearses.

Jackfruit's job in reasonable horticulture reaches out past its ecological and monetary benefits; it likewise holds guarantee as a device for carbon sequestration. As trees, including jackfruit, develop, they retain carbon dioxide from the environment, putting away carbon in their biomass and the dirt. In a period where deforestation and land debasement contribute altogether to ozone depleting substance outflows, the afforestation and reforestation endeavors related with jackfruit development become necessary to worldwide environmental change alleviation methodologies.

The culinary allure of jackfruit further improves its part in economical farming. Past being a nutritious organic product, jackfruit's flexibility in the kitchen positions it as a practical meat substitute. The sinewy surface of unripe jackfruit intently looks like that of meat, going with it a famous decision for veggie lover and vegetarian dishes. The ascent of jackfruit as a meat elective isn't simply a culinary pattern; it tends to the ecological effect related with regular animals cultivating.

The creation of meat, especially hamburger, is connected to deforestation, ozone harming substance emanations, and asset concentrated rehearses. Jackfruit offers a supportable elective that requires less assets, produces less emanations, and diminishes the natural impression related with meat utilization. As buyers progressively look for plant-based options because of ecological worries, jackfruit arises as a critical player in the change toward more economical and moral food decisions.

From a natural viewpoint, the reception of jackfruit as a meat substitute adds to lessening strain on biological systems, checking deforestation, and relieving environmental change. The market interest for plant-based items, including those highlighting jackfruit, makes monetary motivations for ranchers to develop this adaptable harvest. Thus, this encourages the reception of supportable cultivating works on, adjusting horticultural exercises to the standards of ecological protection.

The financial ramifications of jackfruit as a meat elective are significant. For ranchers, the development of jackfruit opens new business sectors and open doors. As the interest for plant-based items rises, the worth of jackfruit as a money crop increments. This financial motivating force benefits individual ranchers as well as adds to the improvement of economical farming practices for a bigger scope. In locales where horticulture is an essential wellspring of business, the combination of jackfruit into cultivating frameworks can possibly elevate networks and upgrade financial versatility.

Jackfruit's part in advancing round economies and waste decrease is one more part of its manageability. The results of jackfruit handling, like strips and seeds, hold undiscovered capacity for different applications. Jackfruit strips, wealthy in fiber and supplements, can be utilized to make biodegradable bundling materials, diminishing the ecological effect of single-use plastics. Jackfruit seeds, frequently disposed of, can be ground into flour or handled to extricate oil, increasing the value of what was once viewed as waste.

Chasing manageability, the usage of jackfruit results embodies the standards of a round economy — a framework where assets are utilized effectively, squander is limited, and items are planned in view of end-of-life contemplations. By bridling the maximum capacity of jackfruit, from organic product to strip to seed, a shut circle framework arises, lessening the ecological impression of the whole worth chain.

As jackfruit ventures from seed to table, its ecological advantages keep on unfurling. The development of jackfruit adds to the protection of biodiversity, the preservation of soil wellbeing, carbon sequestration, and the decrease of waste. Fundamentally, jackfruit typifies the standards of agroecology — a comprehensive way to deal with cultivating that underscores the joining of biological standards into rural frameworks.

The tale of jackfruit as a supportable harvest is a story of interconnectedness. It features the harmonious connection among people and nature, where economical farming turns into a vehicle for ecological stewardship. The flexibility, monetary feasibility, and culinary adaptability of jackfruit make it a strong partner chasing an additional manageable and versatile horticultural future.

All in all, jackfruit's excursion from seed to table isn't simply a gastronomic experience; it is an account of ecological stewardship, monetary strength, and culinary development. As the world wrestles with the difficulties of environmental change, food security, and biodiversity misfortune, jackfruit arises as an encouraging sign — an image of how farming can be changed to address the issues of the present without compromising the prosperity of people in the future. Past its culinary charm, jackfruit remains as a demonstration of the extraordinary force of feasible horticulture in tending to the perplexing and interrelated difficulties confronting our planet.

7.2 Potential economic impact on local communities

The development of jackfruit holds critical commitment for the financial improvement of nearby networks, especially in districts where conventional cultivating faces difficulties from environment fluctuation and monetary vulnerabilities. Jackfruit's financial effect is complex, going from giving manageable kinds of revenue to ranchers to setting out business open doors and adding to in general local area flexibility.

One of the essential monetary benefits of jackfruit development is its low-support nature once the trees are laid out. Dissimilar to some high-support crops that request broad consideration and info, jackfruit trees require insignificant consideration, making them an alluring choice for limited scope ranchers with restricted assets. This low-input, high-yield quality of jackfruit cultivating upgrades its monetary suitability, permitting ranchers to designate their assets all the more effectively and get economical pay from their horticultural undertakings.

The flexibility of jackfruit to different environments further upgrades its financial potential. Jackfruit trees can flourish in different ecological circumstances, from damp tropical areas to drier subtropical zones. This flexibility opens up potential open doors for ranchers in various geological regions to develop jackfruit, consequently differentiating their agrarian exercises and decreasing weakness to the effects of environmental change. The capacity to develop a versatile and versatile harvest like jackfruit adds to the monetary strength of neighborhood networks.

Besides, the financial advantages of jackfruit reach out past the development stage. As the interest for jackfruit and its results increments, it makes new business sectors and monetary open doors for neighborhood networks. The ascent of jackfruit as a meat elective, for instance, has prompted the improvement of significant worth added items, for example, jackfruit-based burgers, wieners, and prepared to-eat feasts. These items take special care of changing buyer inclinations as well as address extra income streams for ranchers and nearby organizations.

The incorporation of jackfruit into neighborhood economies adds to work creation and business open doors. Jackfruit development, collecting, and handling require a workforce, consequently creating work in provincial regions. This viewpoint is especially critical in districts where open positions might be restricted, and horticulture fills in as an essential wellspring of vocation. The business created by the jackfruit esteem chain upgrades the monetary prosperity of neighborhood networks, decreasing joblessness and supporting the general social texture.

The monetary effect of jackfruit isn't restricted to the essential phases of development; it reaches out to downstream exercises and businesses. The handling of jackfruit into different items, like canned merchandise, tidbits, and elements for the food business, sets out open doors for agro-handling organizations. Business visionaries and limited scope endeavors engaged with jackfruit handling add to nearby monetary improvement by enhancing the crude produce and making attractive items for a more extensive customer base.

Moreover, the use of jackfruit side-effects in the formation of biodegradable materials and elective items upgrades financial open doors inside nearby networks. Jackfruit strips, wealthy in fiber and supplements, can be reused for the creation of eco-accommodating bundling materials, diminishing the dependence on traditional plastics. This tends to ecological worries as well as makes new roads for business venture inside the reasonable bundling industry, possibly helping nearby networks monetarily.

The monetary effect of jackfruit additionally stretches out to exchange and business. As the ubiquity of jackfruit develops, it turns into a significant ware for both neighborhood and worldwide business sectors. The commodity of jackfruit and its items adds to unfamiliar trade profit, setting out monetary open doors at a more extensive scale. This exchange potential can upgrade the financial versatility of neighborhood networks by broadening pay sources and lessening reliance on a solitary market or product.

In locales where horticulture assumes a vital part in the economy, the reconciliation of jackfruit into cultivating frameworks can prompt expanded rural efficiency and generally speaking financial development. The financial advantages of jackfruit development echo through the store network, from input providers and ranchers to processors, merchants, and retailers. This interconnected organization of financial exercises cultivates a more unique and versatile neighborhood economy, especially in regions where enhancement is critical for manageability.

Moreover, the monetary effect of jackfruit lines up with more extensive supportability objectives, adding to the improvement of a round economy. By using jackfruit side-effects in the formation of biodegradable materials, elective items, and waste decrease drives, neighborhood networks partake in a round financial model. This model stresses asset effectiveness, squander minimization, and the making of items with an emphasis on maintainability, adjusting financial exercises to natural stewardship.

Taking everything into account, the monetary effect of jackfruit on neighborhood networks is significant and multi-layered. From giving practical kinds of revenue to ranchers to setting out work open doors, supporting agro-handling enterprises, and adding to global exchange, jackfruit arises as an impetus for financial turn of events. Its flexibility, low-support prerequisites, and adaptability in different worth added items position jackfruit as an important resource for nearby economies, cultivating versatility and flourishing notwithstanding monetary difficulties and vulnerabilities. As the worldwide interest for maintainable and plant-based items keeps on rising, the monetary capability of jackfruit presents a chance for nearby networks to fulfill market needs as well as add to an additional economical and fair future.

7.3 The role of Jackfruit in agroforestry and biodiversity

Jackfruit, with its strong and versatile nature, assumes a significant part in agroforestry — a practical land-use framework that joins farming yields with trees to make different and tough environments. Agroforestry incorporates the standards of ranger service and horticulture, trying to advance the advantages got from the two trees and yields. In this unique circumstance, jackfruit arises as a key part, adding to the environmental variety, soil wellbeing, and generally speaking maintainability of agroforestry frameworks.

At the core of jackfruit's part in agroforestry lies its capacity to flourish in assorted environments and soil conditions. Jackfruit trees are appropriate to a scope of conditions, from moist tropical districts to drier subtropical zones. This flexibility makes jackfruit an optimal possibility for consideration in agroforestry frameworks, where different tree species are frequently coordinated to expand natural advantages and improve generally framework strength. By integrating jackfruit into agroforestry plans, specialists can outfit its flexibility to make useful and manageable scenes.

One of the essential commitments of jackfruit to agroforestry is its part in biodiversity preservation. The enormous overhang of jackfruit trees gives shade and living space to different types of birds, bugs, and microorganisms. In agroforestry frameworks, the joining of different plant species, including jackfruit, makes a mosaic of microenvironments that help a wide cluster of greenery. This biodiversity is critical for keeping up with biological system wellbeing, improving irritation control, and elevating generally speaking flexibility to ecological stressors.

Jackfruit's commitment to biodiversity stretches out past its job as a shade tree. The fallen leaves, blossoms, and products of jackfruit trees contribute natural make a difference to the dirt, establishing a supplement rich climate that upholds a different scope of soil microorganisms. This microbial variety is fundamental for soil wellbeing, supplement cycling, and generally speaking environment working. In agroforestry, the consideration of jackfruit upgrades the natural action of the dirt, cultivating conditions helpful for plant development and the prosperity of related vegetation.

The mix of jackfruit into agroforestry frameworks likewise addresses the test of soil disintegration. The broad underground root growth of jackfruit trees helps anchor the dirt, forestalling disintegration and advancing water maintenance. In districts where soil corruption is a huge concern, agroforestry rehearses that incorporate jackfruit add to the preservation of arable land. By moderating soil disintegration, jackfruit assumes an essential part in keeping up with the respectability of horticultural scenes, guaranteeing the drawn out supportability of agroforestry frameworks.

Additionally, jackfruit's job in agroforestry lines up with standards of afforestation and reforestation, adding to carbon sequestration and environmental change relief. As trees, including jackfruit, develop, they retain carbon dioxide from the climate, putting away carbon in their biomass and the dirt. Agroforestry frameworks that integrate jackfruit trees become carbon sinks, balancing ozone harming substance discharges and adding to the worldwide work to battle environmental change. The afforestation and reforestation parts of jackfruit development make it a significant resource chasing reasonable and environment versatile agroecosystems.

With regards to agroforestry, jackfruit's monetary advantages are interlaced with its biological commitments. The development of jackfruit as a component of an agroforestry framework furnishes ranchers with manageable types of revenue. The natural products, seeds, and side-effects of jackfruit handling can be sold in nearby and global business sectors, creating income for ranchers and adding to the monetary practicality of agroforestry rehearses. This financial motivation improves the reception of agroforestry frameworks, guaranteeing their drawn out progress and supportability.

The different cluster of items got from jackfruit increases the value of agroforestry frameworks. While the natural products are a famous and nutritious food source, the seeds can be handled into flour or oil, and the results can be used for biodegradable materials. These worth added items make extra income streams for ranchers participated in agroforestry, advancing the financial broadening of neighborhood networks. The monetary advantages got from jackfruit add to the general achievement and acknowledgment of agroforestry rehearses.

In agroforestry, the spatial course of action of trees and harvests is painstakingly wanted to enhance their cooperations and common advantages. Jackfruit's job as a shelter tree takes into consideration the formation of microclimates underneath its branches, impacting the development and efficiency of understory crops.

Agroforestry frameworks that incorporate jackfruit with reciprocal harvests influence these microclimatic conditions to upgrade generally speaking yields. The cooperative energy among jackfruit and understory crops embodies the potential for agroforestry to give assorted and feasible food creation frameworks.

Moreover, jackfruit's flexibility and strength make it a reasonable contender for agroforestry frameworks in districts inclined to environment changeability. The capacity of jackfruit trees to endure testing conditions, for example, dry season or vacillations in temperature, upgrades the flexibility of agroforestry scenes. As environmental change presents expanding difficulties to customary rural frameworks, the job of agroforestry, with jackfruit as a key part, becomes urgent for building strong and versatile food creation frameworks.

The progress of agroforestry frameworks that consolidate jackfruit depends on sound agroecological standards. Agroecology underscores the joining of biological standards into agrarian works on, zeroing in on the improvement of normal cycles and the advancement of biodiversity. Jackfruit, with its biological flexibility and commitments to biodiversity, adjusts flawlessly with agroecological standards, making it an important resource for professionals looking for manageable and regenerative rural arrangements.

All in all, the job of jackfruit in agroforestry is diverse, enveloping environmental, financial, and social aspects. Jackfruit's flexibility, biodiversity commitments, soil protection benefits, and financial open doors make it a central participant in the improvement of manageable and versatile agroecosystems. As the world wrestles with the difficulties of environmental change, biodiversity misfortune, and food security, the joining of jackfruit into agroforestry arises as a promising arrangement — a demonstration of the capability of nature-propelled, all encompassing ways to deal with horticulture. The cooperative connection among jackfruit and agroforestry represents the interconnectedness of environmental and financial frameworks, offering a pathway toward a more reasonable and agreeable future for horticulture and the planet.

7.4 Future prospects and innovations in Jackfruit cultivation

What's in store possibilities of jackfruit development hold extraordinary commitment, energized by a juncture of variables going from expanding worldwide interest for manageable and plant-based food choices to the intrinsic flexibility and flexibility of the jackfruit tree. As the world wrestles with the difficulties of environmental change, food security, and ecological manageability, jackfruit arises as a strong and diverse arrangement with the possibility to change farming scenes and food frameworks.

One of the vital drivers representing things to come possibilities of jackfruit development is the rising interest for plant-based choices because of ecological and wellbeing concerns. With a developing worldwide populace and expanding consciousness of the ecological effect of conventional meat creation, there is an elevated interest in plant-based counts calories. Jackfruit, with its stringy surface and capacity to emulate the consistency of meat when unripe, stands apart as a convincing meat substitute.

The flexibility of jackfruit in the culinary world positions it as a material for culinary development and imagination. As plant-based counts calories gain notoriety, gourmet specialists and food pioneers are trying different things with jackfruit to make a large number of dishes, from exquisite mains like pulled jackfruit tacos and burgers to sweet treats and bites. The versatility of jackfruit to different flavor profiles and cooking strategies makes it a #1 among those looking for plant-put together options without settling for less with respect to taste and surface.

In the domain of food advancement, the improvement of handled jackfruit items is picking up speed. These items, going from canned jackfruit in saline solution to frozen jackfruit lumps, give helpful choices to shoppers and food producers. Handled jackfruit can be utilized as a base for prepared-to-eat dinners, sauces, and tidbits, extending the span of jackfruit past its conventional structure. The accommodation and flexibility of handled jackfruit items take special care of the requests of occupied ways of life while adding to the mainstreaming of jackfruit in worldwide cooking styles.

As the interest for jackfruit keeps on ascending, there are open doors for esteem expansion and item enhancement. The extraction of jackfruit seeds for flour or oil, for instance, opens roads for the making of new items with nourishing and business esteem. Jackfruit seeds, frequently thought about side-effects, can be tackled for their healthful substance, adding to the improvement of a round economy where waste is limited, and assets are used productively.

Also, the use of jackfruit results in the making of supportable materials is a region ready for advancement. Jackfruit strips, wealthy in fiber and supplements, can be reused for the creation of biodegradable bundling materials. This lines up with the worldwide development towards diminishing single-use plastics and taking on eco-accommodating other options. The crossing point of jackfruit development with economical bundling advancement exhibits the potential for agribusiness to add to more extensive supportability objectives.

With regards to environmental change, the flexibility of jackfruit trees turns out to be progressively huge. Environment versatile yields are significant for guaranteeing food security notwithstanding changing weather conditions, outrageous occasions, and flighty developing circumstances. Jackfruit's capacity to flourish in different environments positions it as a versatile yield that can endure the difficulties related with environmental change, including heat pressure, dry spell, and variances in precipitation.

Agroforestry frameworks that consolidate jackfruit are acquiring consideration as a supportable and environment versatile way to deal with cultivating. The coordination of jackfruit trees with different harvests makes assorted and multifunctional scenes that improve in general environment versatility. Agroforestry gives monetary advantages as well as adds to biodiversity preservation, soil wellbeing, and carbon sequestration. The fate of jackfruit development might consider expanded reception of agroforestry practices to be an all encompassing and regenerative way to deal with farming.

In the mission for manageability, there is a developing interest in agroecology — an all encompassing way to deal with cultivating that underlines the coordination of environmental standards into rural frameworks. Jackfruit's flexibility, low-upkeep necessities, and positive effect on biodiversity make it a reasonable possibility for agroecological rehearses. Agroecology tries to upgrade regular cycles, limit outer information sources, and improve the strength of cultivating frameworks. Jackfruit, with its environmental advantages and flexibility, lines up with the standards of agroecology, offering a dream for a more economical and agreeable fate of farming.

The fate of jackfruit development additionally converges with headways in reproducing and hereditary qualities. Research endeavors pointed toward creating further developed jackfruit assortments with beneficial attributes, like infection opposition, upgraded dietary substance, and further developed yields, can add to the supportability and efficiency of jackfruit plantations. Biotechnological advancements, including hereditary adjustment and genome altering, hold the possibility to speed up the advancement of further developed jackfruit assortments that meet the developing requirements of ranchers and customers.

Besides, the dispersal of information and best practices in jackfruit development is fundamental for augmenting its true capacity. Preparing programs, expansion administrations, and rancher to-rancher information sharing can improve the reception of maintainable and effective jackfruit development rehearses. This information move is especially critical for limited scope ranchers in creating districts, where jackfruit development can assume an extraordinary part in further developing vocations and advancing food security.

The worldwide commercial center for jackfruit and jackfruit items presents the two open doors and difficulties. While expanding request opens roads for market access and monetary open doors, there is a requirement for straightforward and moral stockpile chains. Fair exchange rehearses, confirmations for feasible creation, and adherence to moral work guidelines become significant contemplations to guarantee that the advantages of the developing jackfruit industry are evenhandedly dispersed along the production network.

Moreover, what's in store possibilities of jackfruit development are entwined with exploration and advancement in post-reap innovations. Capacity, handling, and transportation innovations that save the quality and dietary benefit of jackfruit items can broaden market reach and lessen post-gather misfortunes. Developments in bundling, refrigeration, and worth chain foundation are significant for guaranteeing the accessibility of great jackfruit items all year.

Customer mindfulness and schooling assume a basic part in molding the fate of jackfruit development. As jackfruit acquires prevalence as a reasonable and plant-based choice's, how buyers might interpret its healthful advantages, culinary flexibility, and ecological benefits becomes significant. Showcasing endeavors that feature the narrative of jackfruit, its job in manageable farming, and its capability to address worldwide difficulties can additionally push its reception and combination into assorted foods.

All in all, what's in store possibilities of jackfruit development are set apart by a combination of variables — rising interest for manageable food choices, culinary development, flexibility to environmental change, and progressions in agroecology and biotechnology. The flexibility of jackfruit, both in the kitchen and in agroforestry scenes, positions it as a groundbreaking yield with the possibility to add to a more economical and strong food future. As scientists, ranchers, and trailblazers team up to open the maximum capacity of jackfruit, it addresses an encouraging sign in the mission for a regenerative and reasonable horticulture that supports the two individuals and the planet.

Developments in jackfruit development are at the front of changing this tropical organic product into a worldwide horticultural peculiarity. The exceptional properties of jackfruit, combined with headways in innovation, horticultural practices, and supportability, are driving a rush of development that holds guarantee for ranchers, shoppers, and the planet.

One of the critical areas of advancement in jackfruit development lies in reproducing programs pointed toward creating further developed assortments. Customary reproducing strategies, as well as present day biotechnological approaches, are being utilized to improve positive attributes in jackfruit. These qualities might incorporate infection opposition, expanded yield, worked on nourishing substance, and better post-gather attributes. The objective is to make jackfruit assortments that are versatile to natural difficulties as well as meet the advancing requirements of customers and the food business.

Biotechnological developments, for example, hereditary adjustment and genome altering, offer sped up pathways to accomplish explicit enhancements in jackfruit assortments. These advances empower designated changes in the hereditary cosmetics of jackfruit, considering accuracy in improving wanted attributes.

While the utilization of biotechnology in agribusiness raises moral and ecological contemplations, dependable and straightforward use of these apparatuses can add to the improvement of jackfruit assortments with expanded manageability and efficiency.

In lined up with reproducing advancements, accuracy farming is transforming jackfruit development. Accuracy agribusiness includes the utilization of innovation, information, and investigation to enhance different parts of cultivating, including asset use, crop checking, and independent direction. For jackfruit ranchers, accuracy horticulture can improve proficiency in water and supplement the executives, bother control, and generally ranch efficiency. Remote detecting advancements, robots, and sensor organizations can give ongoing information, empowering ranchers to settle on informed choices and answer immediately to evolving conditions.

Environment savvy agribusiness is one more element of advancement in jackfruit development. As environmental change achieves unusual atmospheric conditions and difficulties to customary cultivating rehearses, environment shrewd farming looks to adjust and alleviate these effects. Jackfruit's intrinsic versatility to different environments makes it a reasonable possibility for environment shrewd practices. These may incorporate agroforestry frameworks that improve strength, water-proficient water system strategies, and supportable soil the board rehearses that alleviate the impacts of environment fluctuation.

The combination of jackfruit into agroforestry frameworks is a significant development with various advantages. Agroforestry includes the deliberate mix of trees with harvests or domesticated animals, making expanded and reasonable cultivating scenes. Jackfruit trees, with their huge shelter and versatility, add to the making of agroforestry frameworks that upgrade biodiversity, further develop soil well-being, and give extra monetary open doors to ranchers. The blend of jackfruit with other corresponding yields in agroforestry advances environmental equilibrium and flexibility.

In agroforestry, jackfruit fills in as a multipurpose tree, offering natural products as well as other significant items. The leaves of jackfruit trees can be utilized as feed for domesticated animals, and the wood can be used for different purposes, including development and fuel. The multifunctionality of jackfruit trees in agroforestry lines up with the standards of economical and regenerative agribusiness, where the combination of different components makes tough and useful scenes.

Headways in post-reap advances assume an essential part in guaranteeing the quality and time span of usability of jackfruit items. Gathering, dealing with, and handling advancements add to decreasing post-reap misfortunes and keeping up with the dietary respectability of jackfruit.

Advancements in cool capacity, bundling, and transportation are especially significant in expanding the market reach of jackfruit, permitting it to be appreciated by purchasers all over the planet.

The improvement of significant worth added items got from jackfruit is an eminent development that increases the value of development. Handled jackfruit items, including canned jackfruit, frozen jackfruit lumps, and got dried out jackfruit, give advantageous choices to buyers and food makers. These items take care of changing shopper inclinations as well as make extra income streams for ranchers and add to the mainstreaming of jackfruit in worldwide cooking styles.

In the domain of culinary development, gourmet experts and food lovers are trying different things with jackfruit to make an assorted scope of dishes. From flavorful mains to sweet treats, jackfruit's sinewy surface and gentle taste make it a flexible fixing. Developments in culinary procedures, for example, marinating, smoking, and barbecuing, have raised jackfruit to a status where it can imitate the taste and surface of meat. Jackfruit burgers, tacos, curries, and even treats are becoming famous, adding to the more extensive acknowledgment of jackfruit as a standard fixing.

The use of jackfruit results for manageable designs is an arising area of advancement. Jackfruit seeds, frequently disposed of as waste, can be handled into flour or oil, increasing the value of what was customarily viewed as a result. Jackfruit strips, wealthy in fiber and supplements, can possibly be reused for the production of biodegradable bundling materials. These developments line up with the standards of a roundabout economy, where waste is limited, and assets are used productively.

With regards to maintainable bundling, the advancement stretches out past jackfruit strips. Analysts and business people are investigating the improvement of biodegradable materials utilizing different pieces of the jackfruit plant. The sinewy substance of jackfruit stems and leaves, for instance, can be handled into eco-accommodating options in contrast to traditional bundling materials. These advancements address the ecological effect of single-use plastics and add to the improvement of economical and biodegradable bundling arrangements.

The utilization of advanced stages and online business for advertising and selling jackfruit items is one more road of development. Online stages interface ranchers straightforwardly with customers, setting out open doors for limited scope makers to arrive at a more extensive market. These stages work with the offer of new jackfruit as well as empower the appropriation of significant worth added items, handled products, and results. The direct-to-buyer model cultivates straightforwardness, detectability, and fair exchange rehearses the jackfruit inventory network.

Training and effort drives that influence computerized advances add to the spread of information about jackfruit development. Online courses, online classes, and instructive materials enable ranchers with the most recent data on economical practices, bug the executives, and mechanical headways in jackfruit development.

These computerized assets assume a significant part in building the limit of ranchers, particularly in districts where jackfruit development is acquiring noticeable quality.

Local area based drives and participatory ways to deal with jackfruit development are cultivating advancement at the grassroots level. Rancher cooperatives, local area upheld agribusiness models, and neighborhood networks are instrumental in sharing conventional information, best practices, and advancements. These drives establish a cooperative climate where ranchers can gain from one another, explore different avenues regarding new strategies, and on the whole add to the feasible improvement of jackfruit development.

With regards to worldwide exchange, developments in strategies and store network the board are smoothing out the development of jackfruit items across borders. Cold chain advancements, proficient transportation frameworks, and further developed traditions strategies add to decreasing post-collect misfortunes and guaranteeing the nature of jackfruit items in global business sectors. These advancements open up new open doors for sending out jackfruit and its subordinates, adding to the financial thriving of districts engaged with jackfruit development.

The consolidation of man-made brainpower (simulated intelligence) and information examination into horticulture, generally known as accuracy cultivating, is a groundbreaking development that holds potential for jackfruit development. Artificial intelligence can examine huge datasets, giving bits of knowledge into ideal establishing times, water system timetables, and bug the board techniques. These information driven approaches upgrade decision-production for ranchers, enhance asset use, and add to generally cultivate effectiveness.

www.ingramcontent.com/pod-product-compliance
Lightning Source LLC
LaVergne TN
LVHW020448070526
838199LV00063B/4878